PROVINCIAL FACILITATION FOR INVESTMENT AND TRADE INDEX

# MEASURING ECONOMIC GOVERNANCE FOR BUSINESS DEVELOPMENT IN THE LAO PEOPLE'S DEMOCRATIC REPUBLIC

SECOND EDITION

MARCH 2022

# Contents

Tables, Figures, and Boxes     iv

Foreword     vi

Acknowledgments     viii

Author Profiles     ix

Abbreviations     x

Executive Summary     xi

**1 Introduction**     **1**

**2 Methodology and Respondent Profiles**     **7**

    A. Methodology     8

    B. ProFIT Scoring Methodology     10

    C. Grouping of Provinces for Analytical Purposes     11

    D. Respondent Profiles     12

**3 ProFIT 2019 Index and Survey Results**     **15**

    A. Rankings and ProFIT Index Scores for Large, Medium, and Small Provinces     16

    B. Analysis of Subindex Scores     20

      1. Starting a Business     20

      2. Transparency and Access to Information     22

      3. Regulatory Burden     24

      4. Informal Charges     27

      5. Consistency of Policy Implementation     30

      6. Business Friendliness     35

**4 Selected Policy Issues**     **37**

    A. Enterprise Structure in the Lao PDR     38

    B. Impact of PMO 02/2018 on Business Registration     40

    C. Excessive Cost Burden on Private Businesses     43

**5 Policy Options**     **47**

**Appendix**     **52**

# Tables, Figures, and Boxes

## Tables

1   Comparison of International Assessments for the Lao PDR          2
2   Business Reforms, 2018–2020                                      4
3   Sample Response by Province                                      9
4   ProFIT 2019 Survey Composition and Subindexes                  11
5   Provinces Categorized by Population                             12
6   ProFIT Index 2017 and 2019                                     16
7   Provinces with Official Websites, 2019 and 2022                20
8   Selected Enterprise Indicators, 2006–2020                      38

## Figures

1   ProFIT Index Components                                          8
2   Respondent Profiles                                            13
3   ProFIT Index Scores, 2019                                      17
4   Comparison of ProFIT Index Scores, 2017 and 2019              18
5   Comparison of ProFIT Subindex Scores by Province Size, 2017 and 2019   19
6   Starting a Business in Large Provinces, 2019                   21
7   Cost and Time Required for Business Registration, 2017 and 2019   22
8   Transparency and Access to Information in Provinces, 2019      23
9   Access to Official Documents in Provinces, 2019               24
10  Regulatory Burden in Provinces, 2019                          25
11  Change in Regulatory Burden Score in Provinces, 2017–2019     25
12  Frequency of Inspections in a Year by Provinces, 2019         26
13  Cost and Time Required for Tax Identification Number Renewal in Provinces, 2017 and 2019   27
14  Informal Charges in Provinces, 2019                           28
15  Change in Informal Charges in Large Provinces, 2017–2019      29
16  Consistency of Policy Implementation in Provinces, 2019       31
17  Change in the Policy Implementation Subindex, 2017–2019       31
18  Favoritism toward State-Owned Enterprises in Provinces, 2019  32
19  Advantages of Network Connections in Provinces, 2019          33
20  Consistency of Implementation of National Rules in Provinces, 2019   34
21  Are You Subject to Additional Provincial Rules That Differ from Central Ones?   34
22  Business Friendliness in Provinces, 2019                      35

| 23 | Perception of the Provincial Government in Provinces, 2019 | 36 |
| 24 | Enterprise Structure in the Lao PDR, 2020 | 39 |
| 25 | Enterprises with Necessary Business Documents, 2020 | 39 |
| 26 | Average Cost and Time Required to Complete Business Registration with and without PMO 02/2018 | 40 |
| 27 | Informal Payments during Business Registration, 2017–2019 | 42 |
| 28 | Knowledge on PMO 02/2018 | 42 |
| 29 | Required Pay Informal Charges for Registrations and Licenses | 43 |
| 30 | Average Cost and Time Required to Obtain Operating Licenses | 43 |
| 31 | Cost and Time Required for Compliance for Selected Procedures | 44 |
| 32 | Prevalence of Informal Payments | 44 |

## Boxes

| 1 | Informal Practices in Business Operations in the Lao PDR | 29 |
| 2 | Recent Reforms to Procedures for Starting a Business | 41 |
| 3 | World Bank Assessments of the Business Environment | 45 |
| 4 | Cambodia Online Business Registration System | 46 |
| 5 | Regulatory Reform in Viet Nam | 46 |

# Foreword

The Lao National Chamber of Commerce and Industry (LNCCI) is proud to launch the second Provincial Facilitation for Investment and Trade (ProFIT) Index for the Lao People's Democratic Republic (Lao PDR). The project on the development of this index was financed with technical assistance from the Asian Development Bank (ADB). The ProFIT index aims to measure how well provinces support private sector development, notably through economic governance measures that are under their mandate. ProFIT is a valuable addition to the set of tools with which LNCCI monitors how well provincial authorities facilitate and promote private businesses. It enables the private sector to conduct an informed dialogue with the Government of the Lao PDR.

This ProFIT report draws upon the views of 1,357 enterprises on provincial economic governance in six major categories: (i) ease of starting a business, (ii) transparency and access to information, (iii) regulatory burden, (iv) informal charges, (v) consistency of legal implementation, and (vi) business friendliness of provincial governments. The report shows that the Prime Minister Order No. 02 promulgated in 2018 had a positive impact on the business environment by reducing the cost and time required for business registration. Compared to the first ProFIT survey done in 2017, most provinces recorded better scores in 2019, indicating improved business environment and better local governance.

The outbreak of the coronavirus disease (COVID-19) in 2019 and its subsequent spread across countries had a severe impact on the Lao PDR's economy and the business community. Going forward, overcoming the unprecedented challenges posed by the pandemic will require the central and local governments to work closely with the private sector. That should help design and implement major reforms to reduce the cost and risk of doing business in the Lao PDR, thereby attracting new domestic as well as international investments. The ProFIT 2019 report offers detailed data and analysis on the strengths and weaknesses of the business environment procedures and practices at the local government level.

LNCCI is grateful for the endorsement and support it received from the Ministry of Commerce and Industry and looks forward to continuing strengthening of the policy dialogue. LNCCI is also grateful for the support it received from the Government of Australia and ADB, as well as collaboration offered by the Viet Nam Chamber of Commerce and Industry. We look forward to continued collaboration between the Lao PDR's government and its development partners.

**Oudet Souvannavong**
President
Lao National Chamber of Commerce and Industry

# Foreword

This second Provincial Facilitation for Investment and Trade (ProFIT) Index for the Lao People's Democratic Republic (Lao PDR) follows the first report published in 2018. ProFIT aims to provide a comparative picture of the experiences and perceptions of the business community in complying with government regulations at the subnational level. The second edition of this report notes improvements in the overall business environment across all provinces because of the progress made in the implementation of the formal business registration requirements. However, the report also finds that companies in the Lao PDR remain disadvantaged by excessive regulatory requirements and continuing informal practices. The business environment reforms introduced to date have reduced the cost, but not the prevalence of informal practices, with the incomplete reform agenda impacting tax revenue collection.

A transformative reform agenda on business environment, implemented with efficiency and integrity, is needed to bolster business sentiment to drive a strong post COVID-19 recovery. Speedy implementation of the pandemic recovery, including fresh reforms to improve the business environment, is key for spurring new business opportunities and creating jobs, which will contribute to economic diversification for a more productive future.

The Asian Development Bank is proud to have partnered with the Lao National Chamber of Commerce and Industry in preparing this report. We are equally grateful to the Ministry of Commerce and Industry for its strategic guidance and support throughout the duration of the study.

I sincerely hope that the findings and recommendations included this report are read and discussed widely. If implemented, the ideas contained herein will help to improve the regulatory environment for businesses in the Lao PDR, and in doing so, support a strong private sector-led post-pandemic recovery.

**Ramesh Subramaniam**
Director General
Southeast Asia Department
Asian Development Bank

# Acknowledgments

*Provincial Facilitation for Investment and Trade Index – Measuring Economic Governance for Business Development* was prepared by the Asian Development Bank (ADB) under regional technical assistance project (RETA 9387), Strengthening Institutions for Localizing Agenda 2030 for Sustainable Development, which was generously supported by the Poverty Reduction and Regional Cooperation Fund of the Government of the People's Republic of China. This study was undertaken by the Lao People's Democratic Republic (Lao PDR) Resident Mission (LRM) of ADB. LRM Country Director Sonomi Tanaka provided strategic guidance on the study. The study was completed under the supervision of Senior Country Economist Emma Allen of LRM. Phantouleth Louangraj of LRM and Mai Lin Villaruel of the Macroeconomic Research Division of Economic Research and Regional Cooperation Department provided valuable technical support for the study. Maylee Phommachanh of LRM provided administrative support. Souphavanh Phonmany of LRM provided support for printing and publication request. Srinivasa Madhur led the economic editing of the report. Phan Vinh Quang, independent consultant, and Bounlert Vanhnalat of the National University of the Lao PDR, led the survey of enterprises, including the design of the survey methodology and supervision of the data collection, data analysis, and sharing of preliminary findings with key stakeholders. The data collection team of the Lao National Chamber of Commerce and Industry (LNCCI) consisted of Phouxay Thepphavong, Phonevilay Sinavong, Souphaphone Khamsennam, Daovading Phirasayphithak, Phutthasone Phomvisay, Manitto Phomphothi, Phongsavanh Phetvorlasak, Keomanivone Sayavongsa, Pkoumy Phommivong, Jenjila Chanthasom, Nongthong Vongsavanh, Souphanthong Phonseya, Khamsone Chanthasili, Khonesavanh Chathavong, Lathtekone Sengdeuanphet, and Souksavanh Atsanavong.

Under the guidance of Hanif Rahemtulla and Rachana Shrestha, Marjorie Anne Javillonar, Abigail Armamento, and Rainer Maria Rene Rohdewohld of the Governance Thematic Group at ADB provided support for technical assistance and implementation. This study benefited from invaluable comments received from peer reviewers at ADB, including Gengwen Zhao, Daisuke Mizusawa, and Thuy Trang Dang of the Southeast Asia Department, Robert Lockhart of the Infrastructure Finance Division 2 of the Private Sector Operations Department; Dominic Patrick Mellor of the Office of the Director General of the Private Sector Operations Department; Shawn Tan and Mara Tayag of the Regional Cooperation and Integration Division of the Economic Research and Regional Cooperation Department; and Junkyu Lee of the Sector Advisory Service Cluster-Finance of Sustainable Development and Climate Change Department. ADB's Department of Communications provided a final review and support in printing and the web publication of the report.

This study is a product of extensive consultations with key government ministries in the Lao PDR and their agencies. We are especially grateful to Ministry of Industry and Commerce, Ministry of Finance, and 17 provincial government authorities for their support. We are grateful to advisers of LNCCI, including Siaosavath Savengsuksa, Oudet Souvannavong, Valy Vetsaphong, Xaybandith Rasphone, Bounleuth Luangpaseuth, and Vanthong Sithikoun for their guidance provided throughout the study.

Lastly, we would like to extend our thanks to external stakeholders and partners including Dan Heldon, Hannah Wurf, and Soulivanh Souksavath of the Government of Australia; Painchaud Francois and Anousa Khounnavong of the International Monetary Fund; Tamara Failor of the Asia Foundation; Melise Jaud, Konesavang Nghardsaysone, Alexander Kremer, Sebastian Eckardt, Khampao Nanthavong, Sagita Muco, Nim Vonglatda Omany, and Southida Salaphan of the World Bank; and Aphisid Sengsourivong, Phakpaseuth Lopangkao, Toulakham Phomsengsavanh, Vannaseng Ounalom, Sengphanomchone Inthasane, Sengxay Phousinghoa, and Thipphaphone Vongsay of the Ministry of Industry and Commerce whose insights have been instrumental to the study.

# Author Profiles

**Emma Allen** is a senior country economist at the Lao People's Democratic Republic (Lao PDR) Resident Mission (LRM) of the Asian Development Bank (ADB). Her current responsibilities include heading the economics, strategy, and programming unit of LRM. She prepares the Lao PDR chapter for ADB's flagship publication, *Asian Development Outlook*, as well as ADB's country programming and strategy documents for the Lao PDR. She also supports the design and implementation of ADB loans and technical assistance related to public financial management, reform of state-owned enterprises, sustainable development goals, knowledge and analytical support, and business environment. Prior to joining ADB in 2016, she was a labor market economist with the International Labour Organization. She received her doctor of philosophy (PhD) degree in economics and her bachelor's degree in combined economics and education from the University of Newcastle, Australia in 2015 and 2004, respectively.

**Phantouleth Louangraj** is senior economics officer at LRM of ADB. He is responsible for private sector operations, technical assistance, and knowledge under the economics, strategy, and programming unit of LRM. He administers projects and technical assistance to support private sector development. Prior to ADB, he joined the United Nations Development Programme as project officer. He obtained his master's degree in business administration from Waseda University from Japan in 2004.

**Mai Lin Villaruel** is an economics officer at the Macroeconomics Research Division at the Economic Research and Regional Cooperation Department of ADB. She is part of the team that produces the *Asian Development Outlook* and Asia Bond Monitor. She holds a master's degree in applied statistics from the Macquarie University in Sydney, Australia.

**Srinivasa Madhur,** a former senior director at the ADB, is currently a senior adjunct professor at the Pannasastra University of Cambodia, Phnom Penh, and an economic editorial advisor to ADB's yearly flagship publication, the *Asian Development Outlook.*

**Phan Vinh Quang** is an independent development consultant and has worked on several assignments for ADB, United States Agency for International Development, International Finance Corporation, United Nations Development Programme, Department of Foreign Affairs and Trade (Australia), among others. He helped with partnership between the Vietnam Chamber of Commerce and Industry and the Lao National Chamber of Commerce and Industry on the development of ProFIT in 2017 and 2019. Quang has worked with both the public and private sectors on commercializing technologies, promoting entrepreneurship, value chain development, regulatory reforms, and trade liberalization. He runs a small consulting firm serving international clients in Viet Nam. Quang has a master's degree in business administation from the University of Bath, United Kingdom, and a bachelor's degree from the Foreign Trade University in Viet Nam.

**Bounlert Vanhnalat** is a junior economist in the National University of the Lao PDR, Faculty of Economic and Business Management. Bounlert has a profound research background on international trade and enterprises development in the Lao PDR. He worked as the national consultant to an assessment of the provincial facilitation for investment and trade in the Lao PDR in 2018, and he worked with the Ministry of Industry and Commerce to assess the impact of the Association of Southeast Asian Nations (ASEAN) Economic Community on Lao PDR's economy under the regional economic integration of the Lao PDR into ASEAN and entrepreneurship development. He obtained his PhD degree in economics from the Kobe University, Japan in 2012.

# Abbreviations

| | | |
|---|---|---|
| ADB | – | Asian Development Bank |
| APCA | – | Administrative Procedure Control Agency (Viet Nam) |
| ASEAN | – | Association of Southeast Asian Nations |
| COVID-19 | – | coronavirus disease |
| CEO | – | chief executive officer |
| ERC | – | enterprise registration certificate |
| GCI | – | Global Competitive Index |
| GII | – | Global Innovation Index |
| ICT | – | information and communication technology |
| LNCCI | – | Lao National Chamber of Commerce and Industry |
| MOIC | – | Ministry of Industry and Commerce |
| PMO | – | Prime Minister Order |
| ProFIT | – | Provincial Facilitation of Investment and Trade |
| SOE | – | state-owned enterprise |
| SDG | – | Sustainable Development Goal |
| TAI | – | transparency and access to information |
| TIN | – | tax identification number |
| VAT | – | value-added tax |

**The Provincial Facilitation for Investment and Trade (ProFIT) survey measures and evaluates the recent experiences of enterprises in doing business in the Lao People's Democratic Republic (Lao PDR) at the subnational level.** This report is in its second edition and is based on a survey conducted in 2019 of 1,357 enterprises in 17 provinces across the country. The report focuses on six key areas: (i) ease of starting a business, (ii) transparency and access to information, (iii) regulatory burden, (iv) informal charges, (v) consistency in policy implementation, and (vi) business friendliness of the provincial administration.

**In 2018, the Government of the Lao PDR adopted Prime Minister Order No. 02 (PMO 02/2028) with the aim of improving the country's business environment.** This major countrywide reform sought to improve business registration by providing tax identification numbers (TINs) and business registration certificates at the same time. PMO 02/2018 thus simplified procedures for obtaining business permits. One of the key mandates of the local governments is the percolation of the central government reforms down to the business community. To understand the impact of PMO 02/2018 at the subnational level, respondents to this survey were asked to report (i) the cost and time required for business registration, and (ii) if they received their TINs and business registration certificates at the same time. If a respondent reported that it received its TIN and business registration certificate at the same time, that enterprise was considered to have followed the business registration under PMO 02/2018.

Key finding 1: Between 2017 and 2019, the overall business environment improved across all provinces, pointing to improvement in subnational governance of business operations.

**Most provinces recorded higher scores in 2019 than in 2017 indicating improvement in local business conditions.** The average score of all provinces in the 2019 survey was 55.4 points out of 100, up by 6.6 points from the 2017 figure, but still well below 100, indicating substantial room for further improvement. Following the methodology established in the 2017 survey, results of participating provinces were categorized according to the size of the business units—large, medium, and small.

**Among the 17 provinces covered by this report, Vientiane Province performed the best in 2019 while Champasak was at the bottom of the table.** Vientiane Province recorded the highest score in ProFIT index at 62.6 points and was the best performer on regulatory burden and informal charges. Reduction in the cost and time required for renewing the tax license and fewer business inspections led to the improvements in the province. On an average, informal charges in Vientiane Province were only 3.4% of the enterprise's revenue, lower than country's average of 5.6%, and tax negotiations were not as common in the province. Meanwhile, Champasak scored only 45.8 points, indicating significant scope of improvement in its business environment.

**Savannakhet recorded the largest improvement over time; its ProFIT 2019 score was higher by 15.8 points compared to the 2017 figure**. The province exhibited improvements in all areas of business environment, but especially in terms of consistency of policy implementation and regulatory burden. This is due largely to provincial policy regulations that facilitate its position as a trading hub between the Lao PDR, Thailand, and Viet Nam. Attapu is the only province to score lower in 2019 than in 2017. Attapu's score on business friendliness and transparency and access to information fell by 12.2 and 9.9 points, respectively.

**Key finding 2: Regulatory burden decreased due to consolidation of registration requirements on businesses. However, progress was lethargic in terms of (i) transparency and access to information, (ii) business friendliness, and (iii) informal charges.**

**Improvements occurred across most of the six subindexes of ProFIT, except for access to information.** This relates to the effectiveness of dissemination of regulations, as well as the quality of infrastructure for information communication and dissemination. Almost all the firms reported to having paid informal charges for accessing provincial government documents as well as for business inspections. Most enterprises reported that informal payments were required for ensuring efficient business operations. Among provinces, scores for Oudomxai, Vientiane Province, and Xaignabouli dropped the most. Oudomxai and Xaignabouli, both medium-sized provinces, did not have provincial websites on business procedures. While Vientiane Province tops the list in the overall index, access to information, especially on procurement opportunities and provincial budget, is still on the lower side. Huge bureaucratic reluctance to use internet facilities, even for booking train tickets for the new railway linking the Lao PDR with the People's Republic of China, is a telling example of the constraints on even an otherwise reform-minded new prime minister of the country. The continuing threat of the coronavirus disease (COVID-19) indeed provides an opportunity to the Lao PDR to minimize person-to-person contacts and embrace information technology for delivering many public services.

**Key finding 3: Companies in the Lao PDR remain disadvantaged by excessive regulatory requirements and continuing informal practices.**

**More than two-thirds of enterprises in the country report that they had to pay informal charges to obtain registrations, licenses, and permits.** Tax negotiation practices between enterprises and government officials were found to be widespread across all provinces. This finding indicates that it is complicated, costly, and time-consuming for enterprises to comply with laws, regulations, and procedures that govern the business environment. Louangphabang fared the worst because of its complicated documentation procedures, especially in terms of requirements for operating licenses as well as its failure to disclose formal charges and fees, prompting many entrepreneurs to resort to paying informal charges.

**Key finding 4: Business environment reforms reduced the cost, but not the prevalence of informal practices, with the incomplete reform agenda impacting tax revenue collection.**

**Despite overall improvements noticed in the 2019 survey, firms across the board still incurred substantial informal charges.** This survey shows that the implementation of PMO 02/2018 reduced the cost of business registration by 33.9% and the time required by 37.3%, but the regulation did not remove or reduce the incidence of the practice of enterprises paying informal charges. The high prevalence of informal practices in the business environment, including payments to officials that are not part of formal fees, negotiations of taxes, underreporting of enterprise income, and difficulties in accessing official information, has broader implications for government effectiveness. This hinders the ability of the government to pursue public policies for developing a more competitive private sector and fostering trust in the tax system for higher levels of voluntary compliance. The cumbersome and complex regulatory framework indicates that the Lao PDR has likely forgone substantial tax revenue collections needed for sustaining spending on critical public services. There is thus huge merit in implementing policy measures to make registration and the payment of taxes easier and more effective through automation and at the same time educating and training businesses on how best to use the automated business processes. Such measures could substantially reduce informal charges and improve the business environment. That, in turn, could attract both domestic and foreign investments into the Lao PDR.

Key finding 5: A transformative reform agenda on business environment, implemented with efficiency and integrity, is needed to bolster business sentiment to drive a strong post-COVID-19 recovery.

**Overall, this report notes progress in the procedures and implementation of policy reforms aimed at reducing the hurdles to business development and diversification at the subnational level in the country. Yet, there is substantial scope for further improvement, as has been recognized by the new government itself in its Ninth National Socio-Economic Development Plan for 2021– 2025.** The Lao PDR's economy and business community were hit hard by the COVID-19 pandemic. Overcoming the challenges posed by COVID-19 will require critical reforms to reduce the cost and risk of doing business. The ProFIT index and its subcomponents should provide additional tools to enhance dialogue between private sector and the local governments in the country. This report's findings could also help the governments at all levels in the country in making progress toward the Sustainable Development Goals (SDGs). In particular, it should help the country in achieving SDG 8 on decent work and economic growth and SDG 9 on industry, innovation, and infrastructure. Progress on these SDGs requires implementation of development strategies and policy actions at the subnational level. To support inclusive and equitable private sector development, a separate ProFIT report on gender issues in the business environment is also available.

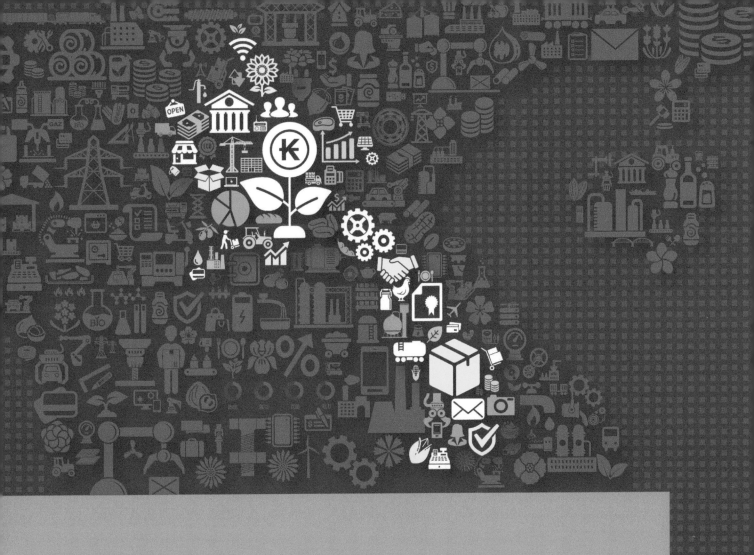

# Chapter 1

## Introduction

There is significant literature on the business environment and investment climate in the Lao People's Democratic Republic (Lao PDR). Analysis by the World Economic Forum in terms of its Global Competitiveness Index (GCI) and the World Intellectual Property Organization using the Global Innovation Index (GII) highlight that the country has made significant progress in its investment climate and business environment. At the same time, these reports point out that substantial scope remains for further policy reforms as well as better implementation of the country's business regulations at the subnational level. The Lao PDR, with a score 50.1 of 100, ranked 113th out of the 141 economies covered in the 2019 GCI report. The GCI report emphasized that cumbersome administrative requirements for starting a business badly impacted business dynamism (Table 1). In the 2021 GII report, the country scored 20.2 of 100, ranking 113th out of 131 economies, with institutional quality impacting on the business environment. Performance on the World Bank's Worldwide Governance Indicators in 2020 also noted significant lacuna in the country's regulatory quality for enabling private sector development.

**Table 1: Comparison of International Assessments for the Lao PDR**

| Global Competitiveness Index 4.0 2019 edition (Percentile rank = 0 lowest, 100 highest) | | Global Innovation Index 2021 (Percentile rank = 0 lowest, 100 highest) | | Worldwide Governance Indicators 2020 (Percentile rank = 0 lowest, 100 highest) | |
|---|---|---|---|---|---|
| Overall | 50.1 | Overall | 20.2 | Voice and accountability | 3.4 |
| Institutions | 42.8 | Institutions | 37.9 | Political stability | 69.3 |
| Infrastructure | 59.2 | Human capital and research | 16.3 | Government effectiveness | 22.6 |
| ICT adoption | 44.2 | Infrastructure | 22.7 | Regulatory quality | 21.2 |
| Macroeconomic stability | 69.7 | Market sophistication | 39.5 | Rule of law | 20.7 |
| Health | 60.9 | Business sophistication | 24.3 | Control of corruption | 14.9 |
| Skills | 51.3 | Knowledge and technology outputs | 6.8 | | |
| Product market | 54.1 | Creative outputs | 17.6 | | |
| Labor market | 57.0 | | | | |
| Financial systems | 55.2 | | | | |
| Market size | 42.1 | | | | |
| Business dynamism | 36.8 | | | | |
| Innovation capacity | 28.0 | | | | |

ICT = information and communication technology, Lao PDR = Lao People's Democratic Republic.
Sources: World Economic Forum; World Intellectual Property Organization; World Bank.

In recent years, the Ministry of Industry and Commerce (MOIC) in the Lao PDR has conducted a series of diagnostic reports on various aspects of the country's business environment and investment climate. These reports focused mainly on the reforms at the central government level. These key findings of these reports included (i) improving access to information on regulations through a portal of inventory of business licenses, (ii) reforms to business operating license inspection requirements, (iii) shift toward a "risk-based" business operating licensing regime, and (iv) empowering the interministerial task force on business environment reform.

The reports from the international institutions provide useful global comparisons, while the reports from the MOIC highlight many domestic issues that both the national and subnational governments in the country will have to address expeditiously for making the investment climate much more business-friendly. For example, the 2019 GCI report finds that the East Asia and Pacific region is the most competitive in the world, but is also home to economies, including the Lao PDR, with significant competitiveness deficits. The report raises major concerns on a whole gamut of issues—the country's long drawn-out dispute settlement process, extensive corruption, inadequacies in corporate governance, limited internet usage, redundancy costs, and time required for starting a business.

The regulatory environment has important implications for diversifying the sources of the country's growth, creation of quality jobs, and expansion of the middle class. It could also enable higher government revenues that are crucial for financing public services. The Lao PDR has many micro- and small enterprises, but not many medium or large enterprises. Informality is high, with 70% of enterprises reporting that they have not registered their businesses. Much of the activity occurs in low-value services, such informal retail trade of food and beverages. Most enterprises do not practice accounting, nor do they use information and communication technology (ICT) tools or have access to finance. Incentives for strong enterprise growth seem lacking, with firm owners reporting that the business environment is one of the biggest hurdles they face.

As a result of the country's comparatively high regulatory burden, noncompliance with rules and standards is common. Many enterprises adopt strategies to avoid attracting government attention, which has implications for investment in innovation required for firms to grow and usher in a vibrant private sector. Overall, ineffective policies on the business environment and a set of weak institutions have contributed to a structure of enterprises that is predominantly informal with low productivity of both capital and labor. Competition-enhancing policies are needed to improve the business environment and foster more firms to innovate and grow. This includes relieving regulatory constraints to incentivize firms to exert efforts to grow, simplification of business registration, and strengthening institutional coordination that would reduce corruption. These measures would create a more predictable and level playing field for firms across provinces.

In addition, location-wise, the Lao PDR is contiguous with Cambodia, Thailand, and Viet Nam. Many businesses could thus choose these neighboring countries too. That is another reason for the country as a whole, and especially those provinces just next to the Lao PDR, to develop a more competitive business environment.

Recognizing these issues, in recent years, the government has issued a range of policies to improve the business environment for enabling the productivity-led growth of enterprises. Since 2018, the Government of the Lao PDR has introduced four major regulatory reforms to enable a more conducive business environment in the country. These reforms seek to streamline business procedures to reduce time and costs for a more speedy, transparent, effective business climate (Table 2). Building on these initiatives, the government has a huge opportunity for deepening reforms and leveraging the private sector to bring in investments to spur the much-needed investments from both domestic and foreign sources. With the commencement of commercial operations of the railway project linking the Lao PDR with the People's Republic of China in December , there is ample opportunity to leverage the new economic opportunities the project may bring in. Now is a critical time for the governments at all levels to strengthen governance and simplify business procedures to enable a private-sector-led economic recovery.

## Table 2: Business Reforms, 2018–2020

| Reforms | Date | Key Measures |
|---|---|---|
| Prime Minister Order (PMO) No.02/PM | 1 February 2018 | **Improvement of Regulations and Coordination Mechanism on Doing Business in the Lao PDR**<br>• Improvement of doing business in the Lao PDR by streamlining procedures and reduce the time and cost required for:<br>» Issuance of enterprise registration certificate and tax identification number at the same time.<br>» Abolishment of the application for authorization to install signage for the enterprise.<br>» Shortening of the import and export approval process by at least 50% in 2019.<br>» Availability of application form for construction permits, including relevant regulations, on the website of the public works and transport.<br>• Implementation of the Investment One-Stop Service mechanism.<br>• Revision and promulgation of the legislation and policies relating to business operations and services.<br>• Harmonization and coordination among government agencies. |
| Prime Minister's Decree No. 3/2019 | 10 January 2019 | **Endorsement of Business Activities under the Controlled Business List and Concession List of the Lao PDR**<br>• Definition of the Controlled Business List and Concession List in the Lao PDR that requires investment license approval:<br>» **Controlled Business List** - list of business activities affecting the national security, the social order, the good and beautiful national tradition and culture and environment, and society and nature to ensure the stable growth of the socioeconomic development.<br>» **Concession List -** list of investor business activities where concession has been approved by the government, mainly land concession, development of special economic zone and industrial processing zones for export, mining, development of energy sources, aviation concession, and telecommunication.<br>• Provision of guidelines and procedures in submitting the application by business activities. |
| PMO No.12/PM | 16 October 2019 | **Facilitation of Import and Export, Temporary Import, Transit and Movement of Goods in the Lao PDR**<br>• Streamlining of the customs clearance process by minimizing time and procedure in importing and exporting of goods.<br>• Implementation of trade regulatory reform by addressing nontariff measures and procedural and/or documentary obstacles faced by private sectors.<br>• Ensuring the implementation of trade facilitation in line with the World Trade Organization Trade Facilitation Agreement. |
| PMO No.03/PM | 21 January 2020 | **Improvement of Services Related to the Issuance of Investment and Business Licenses**<br>• Improvement of platforms, time periods, and obstacles on the issuance of investment and business licenses.<br>• Establishment of a single online database of business licenses, investment licenses, tax registration certificates, and operating licenses among relevant sectors. |

Lao PDR = Lao People's Democratic Republic.
Source: Compiled by Asian Development Bank staff from the Lao Official Gazette, Ministry of Justice (Lao Gazette).

However, the onset of the coronavirus pandemic (COVID-19) in 2019, and its continuation in 2020, 2021, and 2022, has changed the course of the economy. As with countries across the world, the Government of the Lao PDR responded to the pandemic with mobility restrictions that disrupted activities in services and manufacturing. This has had adverse implications for economic growth and public finances.

In response, a national agenda to address the country's economic and financial difficulties was announced in August 2021. However, economic growth is unlikely to recover to pre-pandemic levels in the near term, with projections for real gross domestic product growth not expected to exceed 4.5% in 2022 and 2023. Prospects for recovery are inextricably linked to improvements in the country's health system capacity to administer virus prevention and treatment programs that provide a requisite level of health security in the country, as well as policies to improve investor sentiment for economic recovery. A swift recovery from the pandemic depends on policies that support businesses and households to adapt to the "new normal." This further underscores the need for improving the country's investment climate and business environment.

Encouragingly, the government has identified five core issues that it will focus on to address its economic and financial difficulties in 2021–2023. These include policies to (i) attract trade and investment for promoting economic growth, (ii) strengthen revenue collection and budget execution, (iii) improve economic returns on foreign investments, (iv) manage public debt, and (v) address exchange rate risks and nonperforming loans in the financial system. Related to the business environment, the government plans to remove regulatory barriers faced by enterprises, including removing duplications in the process of investment approvals and improving enforcement and implementation of recent business reforms. The business community and broader private sector expects governments at all levels to significantly reduce the hurdles they face in conducting their activities.

Augmenting the existing studies on business environment in the Lao PDR, this report attempts to (i) provide further evidence and analysis on the business environment, but with a special focus on the implementation of reform measures that are under the purview of the subnational governments; (ii) strengthen the voices of micro, small, and medium-sized enterprises; and (iii) provide recommendations on how the central and subnational governments could help to ease the constraints on businesses in the country. It is expected that the findings of this report would help to promote private sector development by improving the local business environment.

In particular, the report should help strengthen the voices of small and medium-sized enterprises in the Lao PDR about the hurdles they face at the subnational government levels. The report thus does not measure how the provincial business environment is constrained by such factors as infrastructure, labor force and its quality, or the barriers to business arising out of inadequate international trade facilitation, as these are not generally under purview of local governments.

This report uses the ProFIT index derived from the survey to:

(i)  rank provinces in the Lao PDR according to their performance in promoting private sector enterprises;
(ii) analyze individual indicators for a better understanding of the strengths and weaknesses of each province to help promote private business development, and the local governments take the much-needed prompt corrective actions;

(iii) evaluate the local governments' implementation of reforms, and see if they achieve the intended results of improving economic governance, business environment, and the provincial economy; and

(iv) enable provinces to compete for investment by reforming local governance, policies, and policy implementation to develop local economies.

# Chapter 2

Methodology and
Respondent Profiles

## A. Methodology

The report and its findings are based on a survey of 1,357 enterprises in 17 provinces of the country. Within each province, the survey used a simple random sampling approach. The businesses selected were asked to rate their experience and perceptions of the local government under six key metrics: (i) ease of starting a business, (ii) transparency and access to information, (iii) regulatory burden, (iv) informal charges, (v) consistency in policy implementation, and (vi) business friendliness of provincial governments (Figure 1).

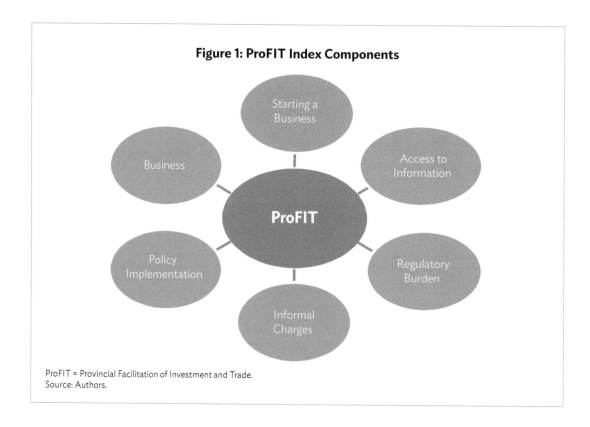

**Figure 1: ProFIT Index Components**

ProFIT = Provincial Facilitation of Investment and Trade.
Source: Authors.

With information on the experiences and perceptions of 1,357 enterprises, the ProFIT 2019 survey is one of the most comprehensive and inclusive surveys for the Lao PDR on the domestic business environment and local economic governance. The findings of the report should help subnational governments to further strengthen the implementation of development policies.

The 2019 survey was conducted from September to December 2019 across 17 provinces in the country. Xaysomboun province, which was established as a province in 2013, was not included in the survey due to the Lao National Chamber of Commerce and Industry (LNCCI) not having established a membership base in the province. The survey included enterprises that were either the members of the LNCCI or newly established units that were registered with the Enterprise Registration Department of the MOIC. In each province, using a simple random sampling, the research team worked with the local LNCCI representatives to randomly select enterprises.

The study team of this report ensured that at least 60 business owners responded in each province. Approximately 60% of the enterprises attended a ProFIT 2019 survey workshop, conducted from 1 October to 6 November 2019. At the ProFIT workshops, chief executive officers (CEOs) of the selected enterprises completed a questionnaire and were invited to share their views on the challenges and opportunities in their local business environments. LNCCI sent online versions of the questionnaire to business owners who could not attend the workshops in person. The enterprises that participated in the ProFIT 2019 survey represented approximately 1.0% of all enterprises as of 2020, with provincial variation from 0.5% in Louangphabang and 4.0% in Xekong (Table 3).

**Table 3: Sample Response by Province**

| Province | Number of Responses Received in 2017 | Number of Invitations Sent in 2019 | Number of Responses Received in 2019 | Response Rate in 2019 (%) | % of All Government Registered Businesses | % of All Enterprises Survey |
|---|---|---|---|---|---|---|
| Vientiane Capital | 314 | 350 | 306 | 87.4 | 0.7 | 22.5 |
| Phongsali | 50 | 100 | 60 | 60.0 | 3.3 | 4.4 |
| Louangnamtha | 50 | 100 | 61 | 61.0 | 2.3 | 4.5 |
| Oudomxai | 50 | 100 | 60 | 60.0 | 1.3 | 4.4 |
| Bokeo | 50 | 100 | 60 | 60.0 | 1.3 | 4.4 |
| Louangphabang | 75 | 120 | 70 | 58.3 | 0.5 | 5.2 |
| Houaphan | 64 | 100 | 60 | 60.0 | 1.2 | 4.5 |
| Xaignabouli | 57 | 100 | 64 | 64.0 | 0.8 | 4.8 |
| Xiangkhouang | 68 | 100 | 66 | 66.0 | 0.8 | 4.9 |
| Vientiane Province | 78 | 120 | 81 | 67.5 | 0.7 | 6 |
| Bolikhamxai | 61 | 100 | 66 | 66.0 | 1.3 | 4.8 |
| Khammouan | 55 | 100 | 62 | 62.0 | 1.1 | 4.6 |
| Savannakhet | 80 | 120 | 80 | 66.7 | 0.9 | 5.9 |
| Salavan | 50 | 100 | 61 | 61.0 | 1.2 | 4.5 |
| Xekong | 55 | 100 | 60 | 60.0 | 4 | 4.4 |
| Champasak | 74 | 120 | 80 | 66.7 | 0.7 | 5.9 |
| Attapu | 50 | 100 | 60 | 60.0 | 3 | 4.4 |
| **Total** | **1,281** | **2,030** | **1,357** | **66.8** | **1** | **100** |

Source: Authors.

The ProFIT 2019 questionnaire consisted of an introductory section followed by questions under each of the six subtopics. The introductory questions asked respondents to provide general information on their businesses, including type, size, gender of the CEO, and professional, background. The 2019 questionnaire was updated from its 2017 version to elicit more detailed information on gender and time taken to complete certain business procedures. Instead of asking respondents to select from a range of multiple-choice answers, the 2019 survey required respondents to provide specific numerical answers regarding costs, times, and other indicators (Appendix).

This report compares the scores and ranks of each province across other provinces as well as with the results of the 2017 ProFIT survey. The 2017 survey covered all the 17 provinces, but the survey included a lower number of business units, with a sample of 1,281. The business units covered in the 2019 survey are the not the same as the ones covered in the 2017 survey, although the two surveys may include business units that overlap the two surveys. Thus, the data and the comparison of results between the two surveys are not drawn from a panel data set. As such, the temporal comparisons are subject to some limitations. Nevertheless, it provides an approximate idea of how the business environment changed between 2017 and 2019.

The 2019 survey questionnaire has a few minor changes from the 2017 version, with further information collected on starting a business and business friendliness. In the 2017 questionnaire, the score for starting a business was based only on the cost and time required to complete business registration. The 2019 scoring approach maintains this methodology for comparison. However, further questions on the cost and time required to obtain business operating licenses after obtaining a business registration were added to the survey questionnaire.[1] These results are shared in this report.

Lastly, the publication of this report has been delayed by the onset of the COVID-19 pandemic. The data captured in the report provides a snapshot of the experiences with businesses in the implementation of PMO 02/2018 at the end of 2019. With time, the reform implementation should have gathered further momentum and further policy reforms may have helped to advance the agenda. Equally, it is likely there may be setbacks related to the pandemic that may have stalled reform implementation at the subnational level. For instance, in 2019, 11 of 17 provinces had operating provincial websites. In 2022, this had reduced to only seven. In this regard, it would be timely to complete a third round of data collection.

## B. ProFIT Scoring Methodology

The ProFIT index is made up of six subindexes, each with an equal weight of 16.7% of the total score. Each subindex is computed based on responses on several questions from the questionnaire. Answers to each question in the survey were scored from 0 to 100 points, with zero as the lowest or worst and 100 as the highest or the best, and provincial results were measured against a perfect score to arrive at each province's "distance to the frontier." Extreme outliers were eliminated from the data set before the survey results were tabulated.

Using the survey results, provinces are ranked by their scores on six subindexes (i) starting a business, (ii) transparency and access to information, (iii) the regulatory burden, (iv) formal and informal charges, (v) consistency in implementing laws, and (vi) the provincial government's attitude toward business (Table 4). These areas are selected because subnational governments have the mandate to implement regulations covering these aspects of business environment. Issues relating to foreign trade facilitation—a key component of overall business environment of a country—is not included in this report, as it falls mostly under the mandate of the central government.

---

[1]    Louangphabang, for example, has more tourist businesses that need to apply for tourism licenses, while Xekong has more farming businesses that need operating licenses in agriculture.

**Table 4: ProFIT 2019 Survey Composition and Subindexes**

| Subindex | % | Indicator | % |
|---|---|---|---|
| 1. Starting a business | 100 | Business registration time | 50 |
| | | Business registration cost | 50 |
| 2. Transparency and access to information | 100 | Access to provincial documents | 60 |
| | | Provincial websites | 20 |
| | | Opportunity to comment on draft regulations | 20 |
| 3. Regulatory burden | 100 | Inspections by authorities | 30 |
| | | Tax registration certificate renewal time | 35 |
| | | Tax registration certificate renewal cost | 35 |
| 4. Informal charges | 100 | Informal charges as a share of revenue | 40 |
| | | Acceptability of informal charges | 15 |
| | | Commonality of tax negotiations | 15 |
| | | Necessity of informal charges | 15 |
| | | Public disclosure of formal charges | 15 |
| 5. Consistency of implementation | 100 | Advantages of personal connections | 20 |
| | | Favoritism for state-owned enterprises | 20 |
| | | Consistency of regulations with national rules | 20 |
| | | Internal coordination to support business | 20 |
| | | Provincial regulations differ from national ones | 20 |
| 6. Business friendliness | 100 | Attitude of provincial government | 25 |
| | | Helpfulness of provincial government | 25 |
| | | Application of new solutions to solve problems | 25 |
| | | Knowledge of PMO 02/2018 | 25 |

PMO = Prime Minister Order.
Source: Authors.

## C. Grouping of Provinces for Analytical Purposes

Challenges and opportunities for enterprises in the country vary widely across provinces. In a large province, enterprises must deal with bureaucracies that overburden them with numerous business applications, whereas in smaller provinces local officials themselves may be far less familiar with regulations. Based on early extensive consultations with LNCCI and its continued involvement with the study, the study team divided provinces into three categories: (i) small provinces with populations of 100,000–200,000 people, (ii) medium provinces with 200,000–400,000 people, and (iii) large provinces with over 400,000 people (Table 5).

**Table 5: Provinces Categorized by Population**

| Large Provinces | Population >400,000 |
|---|---|
| Savannakhet | 969,697 |
| Vientiane Capital | 820,940 |
| Champasak | 694,023 |
| Louangphabang | 431,889 |
| Vientiane Province | 419,090 |
| **Medium Provinces** | **Population 200,000–400,000** |
| Salavan | 396,697 |
| Khammouan | 392,052 |
| Xaignabouli | 381,376 |
| Oudomxai | 307,622 |
| Houaphan | 289,393 |
| Bolikhamxai | 273,691 |
| Xiangkhouang | 244,684 |
| **Small Provinces** | **Population <200,000** |
| Bokeo | 179,243 |
| Phongsali | 177,989 |
| Louangnamtha | 175,753 |
| Attapu | 139,628 |
| Xekong | 113,048 |

Sources: Population and Housing Census 2014.


## D. Respondent Profiles

The 1,357 participants in the ProFIT 2019 survey were drawn from the 17 provinces in the country with each province providing at least a 60% response rate, except for Louangphabang providing just a bit lower response rate of 58.3%. The survey results were tabulated by sector, age, gender of the CEO, and enterprise size (Figure 2). Micro, small, and medium-sized enterprises accounted for 93.5% of survey participants while 6.5% of respondents were from large enterprises. By sector, 80.6% were in manufacturing, services, or trading activities. About 34% were established between 2015 and 2019. According to the 2020 Economic Census III, medium enterprises with 51–99 employees account for only 0.7% of enterprises in the Lao PDR while large enterprises (100+) account 0.2% of enterprises. This implies that the ProFIT data is likely to be slightly biased toward larger enterprises, as the survey sample captures a larger share of these enterprises.

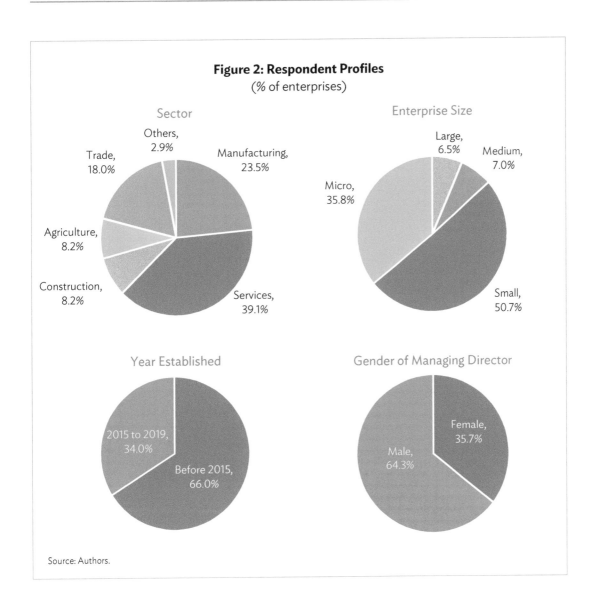

**Figure 2: Respondent Profiles**
(% of enterprises)

*Source: Authors.*

The survey questionnaire was revised to include questions on the gender of the CEOs and if female shareholders owned 30% or more of enterprise's equity. About 36% of respondents said their CEOs were female. This is somewhat similar to the 2020 Economic Census III, which found that 43.8% of the surveyed enterprises have female managers or directors.[2]

---

2    A separate report will be published on analysis of enterprises' "gender and provincial facilitation for investment and trade index." This report thus attempts to use these data to analyze potential gender implications in the local economic governance and business environment.

# Chapter 3

ProFIT 2019 Index
and Survey Results

## A. Rankings and ProFIT Index Scores for Large, Medium, and Small Provinces

The average score for all provinces in the ProFIT 2019 survey is 55.4, which is 6.6 percentage points higher than the average score in 2017, pointing to some improvements in the business environment in the country. Except for Attapu province, all provinces achieved higher ProFIT scores in 2019 than in 2017 (Table 6).

**Table 6: ProFIT Index 2017 and 2019**

| Provinces | ProFIT Score | | |
|---|---|---|---|
| | 2019 | 2017 | Change |
| **Large** | **53.7** | **44.1** | **9.6** |
| Louangphabang | 49.2 | 38.6 | 10.6 |
| Vientiane Province | 62.6 | 53.8 | 8.8 |
| Vientiane Capital | 52.4 | 46.2 | 6.2 |
| Savannakhet | 58.8 | 43.0 | 15.8 |
| Champasak | 45.8 | 39.1 | 6.7 |
| **Medium** | **57.8** | **51.4** | **6.5** |
| Oudomxai | 56.6 | 55.1 | 1.5 |
| Houaphan | 59.9 | 54.4 | 5.5 |
| Xaignabouli | 59.4 | 50.5 | 8.9 |
| Xiangkhouang | 59.0 | 55.7 | 3.3 |
| Bolikhamxai | 54.5 | 49.9 | 4.6 |
| Khammouan | 54.9 | 45.0 | 9.9 |
| Salavan | 60.5 | 48.9 | 11.6 |
| **Small** | **53.6** | **49.9** | **3.7** |
| Phongsali | 57.4 | 51.6 | 5.8 |
| Louangnamtha | 54.5 | 43.8 | 10.7 |
| Bokeo | 52.9 | 51.4 | 1.5 |
| Xekong | 55.2 | 48.9 | 6.3 |
| Attapu | 47.9 | 53.7 | -5.8 |
| **Overall** | **55.4** | **48.8** | **6.6** |

ProFIT = Provincial Facilitation of Investment and Trade.
Source: Authors.

Large provinces tended to have the greatest variation in their scores, reporting both the highest and the lowest scores. (Figure 3).

- **Large provinces.** Vientiane Province topped the list scoring 62.6 points, followed by Savannakhet at 58.8 points, while Champasak was at the bottom with a score below 50.
- **Medium provinces.** Salavan scored the highest score 60.5, followed by Houaphan, Xaignabouli, and Xiangkhouang—all scoring about 60.0 points. Bolikhamxai is at the bottom with a score of 54.5.

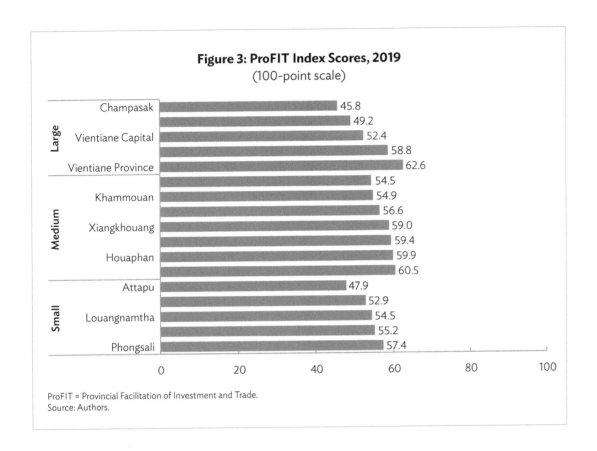

**Figure 3: ProFIT Index Scores, 2019**
(100-point scale)

ProFIT = Provincial Facilitation of Investment and Trade.
Source: Authors.

- **Small provinces.** Phongsali had the highest score of 57.4, followed by Xekong, Louangnamtha, and Bokeo. Attapu scored less than 50 points, despite having ranked first among small provinces in the ProFIT 2017 Index.

Private sector perceptions of Attapu's business environment deteriorated between 2017 and 2019 across all areas covered by this report. The subindex with the biggest drop is on perceptions of local government's business friendliness, with 60% of respondents from the province perceiving that the provincial government performed far below their expectations in terms of facilitating private sector development.

Encouragingly, except for Attapu, all provinces improved their business environment in 2019 compared to 2017 (Figure 4). Attapu's performance was dragged down because of a combination of lengthy durations and high costs of business registration, combined with more frequent inspections by various authorities in comparison to other provinces.

- **Large provinces.** Business perceptions of the local governments' policy environment improved significantly, with that of Savannakhet posting the largest improvement and that of Vientiane Capital witnessing the least improvement.
- **Medium provinces.** These provinces saw an average increase in their score by 6.5 points between 2017 and 2019. Salavan saw the largest improvement and Oudomxai the least.
- **Small provinces.** These provinces witnessed improvements, with Louangnamtha leading, followed by Xekong, Phongsali, and Bokeo.

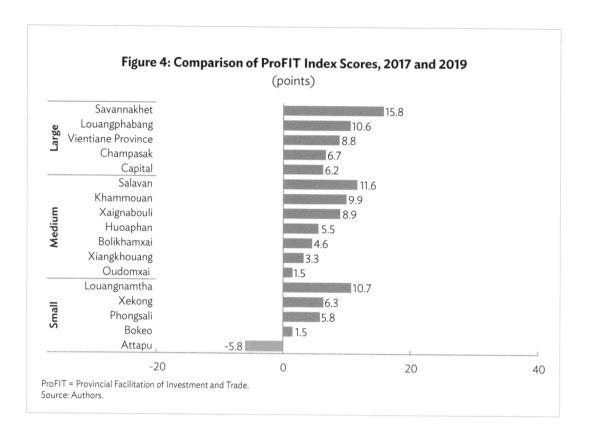

**Figure 4: Comparison of ProFIT Index Scores, 2017 and 2019**
(points)

ProFIT = Provincial Facilitation of Investment and Trade.
Source: Authors.

Prime Minister Order No. 02 in February 2018 (PMO 02/2018) was issued to lighten the regulatory burden on enterprises by removing some unnecessary documentation requirements. That said, substantial variations are still the norm across provinces in this aspect of the ProFIT scores. Progress has also been lackluster on transparency and access to information (Figure 5). This continues to be a recurring theme across most of the 1,357 business firms surveyed for this study.

- **Large provinces.** Improvements were observed in terms of easing the regulatory burden of businesses, followed by consistency of policy implementation, while smaller gains were made on business friendliness and informal charges. Among the six subindexes, transparency and access to information deteriorated between 2017 and 2019.
- **Medium provinces.** Gains were noted in all areas of business environment except in terms of transparency and access to information. The greatest improvements were in terms of the consistency of implementation, up by 16.8 percentage points, followed by regulatory burden, up by 14.4 points from 2017 to 2019. By contrast, the medium provinces reported a slide in terms of transparency and access to information.
- **Small provinces.** Scores improved in terms of consistency in policy implementation, easing regulatory burden, and starting a business but the perception of these firms about local governments' business friendliness, transparency, and access to information and informal charges took a beating.

Insufficient access to provincial documents, such as development planning and procurement opportunities, and lack of transparency continues to be hurdles for firms in doing business, despite 11 out of 17 provinces having set up official websites that are intended to clarify business processes (Table 7). By 2022, the number of provinces with operational provincial websites had decreased to seven.

**Figure 5: Comparison of ProFIT Subindex Scores by Province Size, 2017 and 2019**

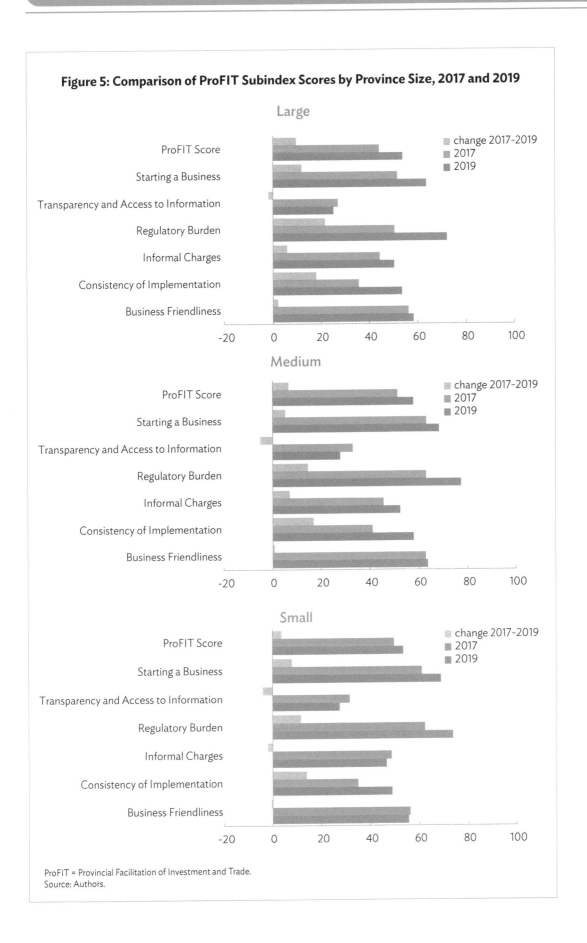

ProFIT = Provincial Facilitation of Investment and Trade.
Source: Authors.

**Table 7: Provinces with Official Websites, 2019 and 2022**

| Size | Name | 2019 | 2022 |
|---|---|---|---|
| **Large** | | | |
| | Louangphabang | No | No |
| | Vientiane Province | Yes | Yes: https://vtpv.gov.la/ |
| | Vientiane Capital | Yes | Yes: http://vientianecity.gov.la/ |
| | Savannakhet | Yes | Not working |
| | Champasak | No | No |
| **Medium** | | | |
| | Oudomxai | No | Yes: https://www.oudomxai.gov.la/ |
| | Houaphan | Yes | Yes: http://houaphan.gov.la/ |
| | Xaignabouli | No | No |
| | Xiangkhouang | No | No |
| | Bolikhamxai | Yes | Yes: http://bolikhamxay.gov.la/ |
| | Khammouan | Yes | Not working |
| | Salavan | Yes | Not working |
| **Small** | | | |
| | Phongsali | Yes | Not working |
| | Louangnamtha | No | No |
| | Bokeo | Yes | Not working |
| | Xekong | Yes | Yes: http://xekong.gov.la/ |
| | Attapu | Yes | Yes: http://attapu.gov.la/ |

Source: The Prime Minister's Office, The Lao People's Democratic Republic. http://www.laogov.gov.la.

# B. Analysis of Subindex Scores

## 1. Starting a Business

The subindex on starting a business measures the cost and time required to register a business but does not include the time it takes to actually start business operations or fully comply with all requirements, such as social security registration (Figure 6).

- **Large provinces.** Vientiane Province scored the highest in terms of starting a business, at 74.6, followed by Savannakhet with a score of 68.1. In contrast, Vientiane Capital ranked lowest with a score of 55.8.
- **Medium provinces.** Salavan, Xaignabouli, Xiangkhouang, and Oudomxai all scored above 70 points out of 100 in this subindex. Khammouan had the lowest score at 59.2 points, while Bolikhamxai scored about 60 points.
- **Small provinces.** Louangnamtha performed the best with score of 82.0 points, while Attapu scored the least with score of 60.9 points.

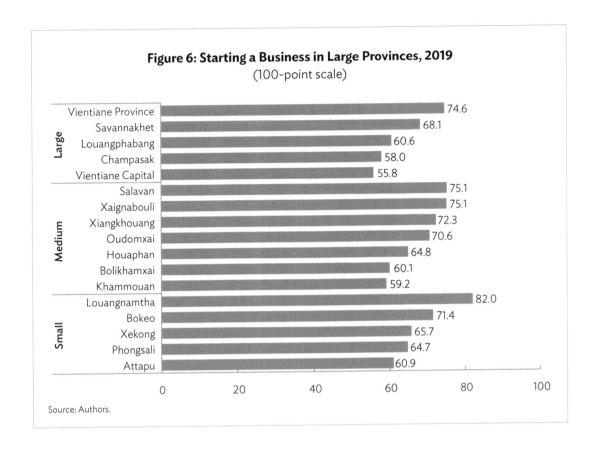

**Figure 6: Starting a Business in Large Provinces, 2019**
(100-point scale)

| | | |
|---|---|---|
| **Large** | Vientiane Province | 74.6 |
| | Savannakhet | 68.1 |
| | Louangphabang | 60.6 |
| | Champasak | 58.0 |
| | Vientiane Capital | 55.8 |
| **Medium** | Salavan | 75.1 |
| | Xaignabouli | 75.1 |
| | Xiangkhouang | 72.3 |
| | Oudomxai | 70.6 |
| | Houaphan | 64.8 |
| | Bolikhamxai | 60.1 |
| | Khammouan | 59.2 |
| **Small** | Louangnamtha | 82.0 |
| | Bokeo | 71.4 |
| | Xekong | 65.7 |
| | Phongsali | 64.7 |
| | Attapu | 60.9 |

Source: Authors.

Enterprises reported that the cost and time required to register a business was lower in 2019 than in 2017 (Figure 7). This is potentially a positive signal for business and may encourage more businesses to formally register their activities. The official fees charged for obtaining an enterprise registration certificate was equivalent to KN590,000 in 2017 and 2019. There was no charge for obtaining a tax identification number (TIN). However, many enterprises still pay large amounts of informal fees, often exceeding double or triple the value of formal fees, for expediting issuance of compliance documentation across the country.

- **Large provinces.** About 22% of the enterprises registered in 2019 reported that they were able to complete their business registration in less than 10 days, improving upon the 6.7% figure for 2017. Two-thirds of the large provinces that registered in 2019 paid KN2 million or less for business registration.
- **Medium provinces.** Half of the respondents reported that they were able to complete their business registration in less than 10 days in 2019, double the 25% figure in 2017. Ninety percent of enterprises established in 2019 paid KN2 million or less for business registration.
- **Small provinces.** In 2019, 40% of small business units reported that it took less than 10 days to complete business registration. About two-thirds of the small enterprises paid KN2 million or less in 2019, much lower than in 2017.

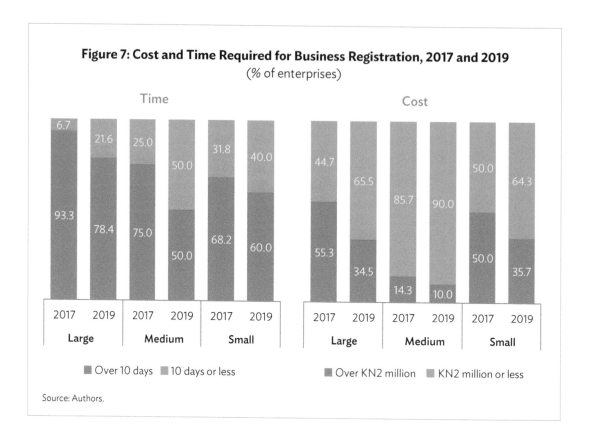

**Figure 7: Cost and Time Required for Business Registration, 2017 and 2019**
(% of enterprises)

Source: Authors.

## 2.   Transparency and Access to Information

Transparency and access to information (TAI) is measured by three indicators: (i) access to provincial documents, (ii) opportunity for businesses to comment on draft regulations, and (iii) timely availability of provincial websites. All provinces had low scores on this subindex (Figure 8). The low scores largely reflected a lack of official websites in these provinces, preventing enterprises from accessing official information on economic planning, procurement opportunities, and other business rules and regulations. It also reflects a lack of an integrated national one-stop window portal for enterprises to apply for registration, licenses, and permits easily and efficiently across provinces. The existing information asymmetries impose a significant transaction cost for the private sector in starting a business.

- **Large provinces.** Vientiane Province performed the best, while Champasak and Louangphabang were at the bottom reflecting the lack of provincial websites.
- **Medium provinces.** Houaphan performed the best with a score of 38.9, followed by Khammouan with a score of 35.8, while Xiangkhouang, Oudomxai, and Salavan, were at the bottom of the table with less than a score of 25.
- **Small provinces.** Phongsali performed the best with score of 32.7 points. Louangnamtha posted the lowest TAI score, just 21.6 points, due largely to the absence of an official website.

Provinces that had set up functioning websites posted improvements in terms of access to information between 2017 and 2019. The fact that many provinces have not yet set up functioning websites indicates that there is huge scope for improving the business environment across many provinces in the country.

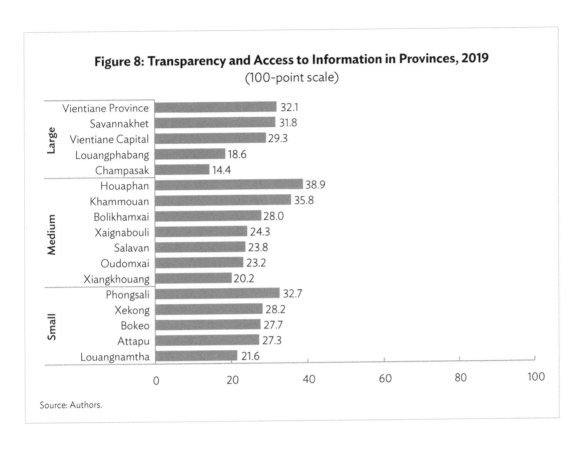

**Figure 8: Transparency and Access to Information in Provinces, 2019**
(100-point scale)

| Category | Province | Value |
|---|---|---|
| Large | Vientiane Province | 32.1 |
| | Savannakhet | 31.8 |
| | Vientiane Capital | 29.3 |
| | Louangphabang | 18.6 |
| | Champasak | 14.4 |
| Medium | Houaphan | 38.9 |
| | Khammouan | 35.8 |
| | Bolikhamxai | 28.0 |
| | Xaignabouli | 24.3 |
| | Salavan | 23.8 |
| | Oudomxai | 23.2 |
| | Xiangkhouang | 20.2 |
| Small | Phongsali | 32.7 |
| | Xekong | 28.2 |
| | Bokeo | 27.7 |
| | Attapu | 27.3 |
| | Louangnamtha | 21.6 |

Source: Authors.

This study went through eight official documents that were considered important for businesses to access at the provincial levels: (i) provincial budgets, (ii) socioeconomic development plans, (iii) regulations and guidelines, (iv) investment budgets for infrastructure development, (v) strategic land-use plans, (vi) investment promotion policies, (vii) procedures and forms, and (viii) public procurement opportunities. Most enterprises lacked access to these eight official documents that are important for business operations (Figure 9).

- **Large provinces.** Although Vientiane Province performed the best in this category of firms, Savannakhet also reported that more enterprises could easily access the provincial-level documents.
- **Medium provinces.** While 39.2% of enterprises in Houaphan reported that they had access to these documents, the figure was lower than 25% in Salavan and Bolikhamxai.
- **Small provinces.** While 29.4% of respondents in Louangnamtha said that they had access to provincial-level documents, barely half as many respondents in Attapu said the same.

It will remain difficult for provincial governments to disseminate official information to the private sector without setting up and regularly updating these websites. An integrated national one-stop portal window that compiles subnational regulations may offer the best solution for efficient access to information by the businesses across provinces. If information is available, it may also reduce the informal transaction charges and foster competition among firms. That could ultimately benefit the society in terms of higher economic growth and better development.

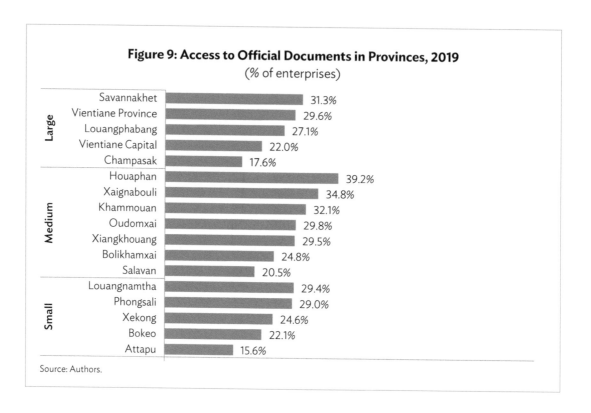

**Figure 9: Access to Official Documents in Provinces, 2019**
(% of enterprises)

| Category | Province | Value |
|---|---|---|
| Large | Savannakhet | 31.3% |
| Large | Vientiane Province | 29.6% |
| Large | Louangphabang | 27.1% |
| Large | Vientiane Capital | 22.0% |
| Large | Champasak | 17.6% |
| Medium | Houaphan | 39.2% |
| Medium | Xaignabouli | 34.8% |
| Medium | Khammouan | 32.1% |
| Medium | Oudomxai | 29.8% |
| Medium | Xiangkhouang | 29.5% |
| Medium | Bolikhamxai | 24.8% |
| Medium | Salavan | 20.5% |
| Small | Louangnamtha | 29.4% |
| Small | Phongsali | 29.0% |
| Small | Xekong | 24.6% |
| Small | Bokeo | 22.1% |
| Small | Attapu | 15.6% |

Source: Authors.

## 3.   Regulatory Burden

The regulatory burden on businesses is measured by three indicators: frequency of inspections by government agencies, the time required to renew a company's TIN, and the cost of TIN renewal (Figure 10). These are not the only regulatory burdens on businesses in the Lao PDR. As such, a high score in the regulatory burden subindex does not necessarily indicate that businesses consider their regulatory burden to be light. Rather, it is simply a relative ranking among the provinces based the three indicators for this subindex.

- **Large provinces.** Vientiane Province had the least regulatory burden, while Champasak had the most regulatory burden.
- **Medium provinces.** Houaphan performed the best, while Oudomxai was at the bottom of the table.
- **Small provinces.** All small provinces scored high in this subindex, with Xekong leading the list with a score of 78.9, followed by Louangnamtha, and Bokeo. Attapu came in at the bottom with a score of 60.8 points.

The regulatory burden on enterprises improved somewhat from 2017 to 2019 (Figure 11). Local enterprises listed less-frequent inspections and reduced time and cost for renewing TINs as the main reasons for the higher scores they reported.

- **Large provinces.** Louangphabang showed significant improvement by 31.0 points, followed by Savannakhet, improving by 26.9 points.
- **Medium provinces.** Khammouan jumped up by 26.4 points. This improvement resulted from the reduced frequency of inspections and of the cost and time that business owners said were required to renew their TINs.

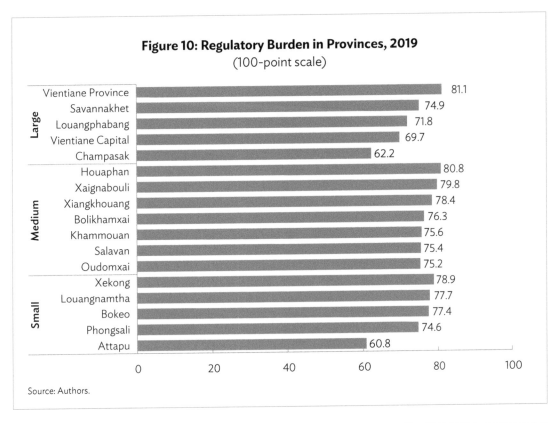

**Figure 10: Regulatory Burden in Provinces, 2019**
(100-point scale)

Source: Authors.

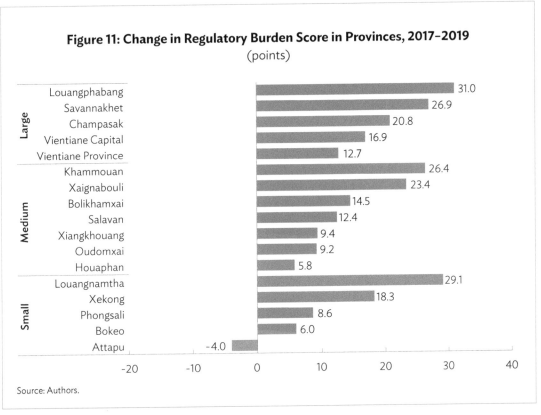

**Figure 11: Change in Regulatory Burden Score in Provinces, 2017–2019**
(points)

Source: Authors.

- **Small provinces.** Louangnamtha is the most improved province in terms of regulatory burden, boosting its score by 29.1 points from 2017 to 2019, as it reined in the cost and time required to renew TINs and simultaneously reduced the frequency of inspections. Attapu has been the exception, posting a lower score in easing regulatory burden in 2019 than in 2017.

A major reason for the slow pace of improvement was the frequency in government inspections (Figure 12). Inspections impose significant time and resource burdens on enterprises, taking time away from enterprise management and creating opportunities for rent-seeking.

- **Large provinces.** In Vientiane Province, 75% of the enterprises were inspected only once or twice in 2018. By contrast, 62.7% of enterprises in Champasak reported being inspected at least three times a year.
- **Medium provinces.** In Khammouan, over 60% of enterprises reported being inspected more than twice in 2018, while 77.4% of enterprises in Houaphan were inspected only once or twice in 2018.
- **Small provinces.** More than 80% of businesses in Attapu reported that they were inspected at least thrice in 2018, as did nearly two-thirds of enterprises in Phongsali.

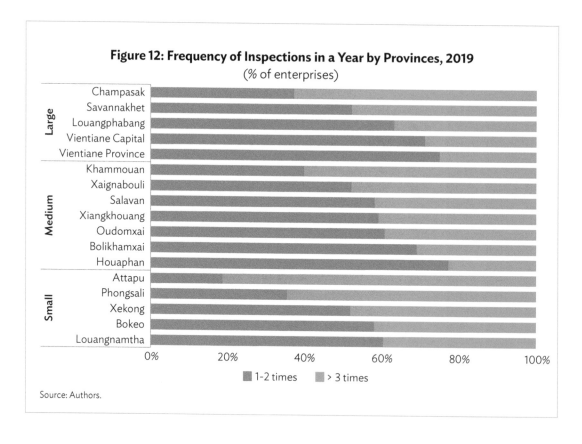

**Figure 12: Frequency of Inspections in a Year by Provinces, 2019**
(% of enterprises)

Source: Authors.

Enterprises are still required to renew TINs annually, entailing substantial time and cost for businesses. The cost and time required for enterprise's TIN renewal processes reduced, but enterprises still report that the process requires about a month to complete (Figure 13). TIN annual renewal takes an average of 16 days and costs about KN2.0 million, although one in four enterprises reported paying more than KN3 million for TIN renewal. There would thus be huge merit in abolishing the requirement of an annual renewal of TINs.

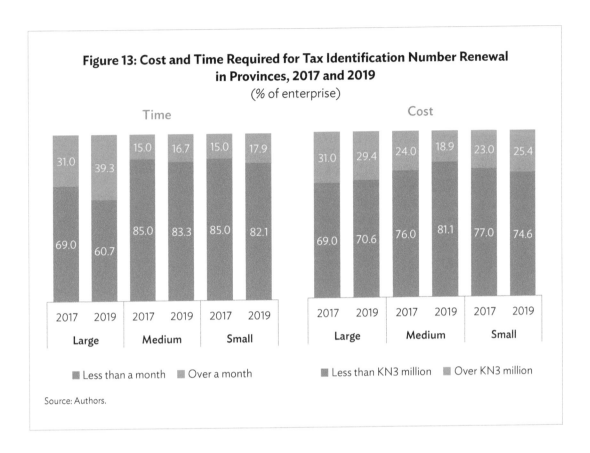

**Figure 13: Cost and Time Required for Tax Identification Number Renewal in Provinces, 2017 and 2019**
(% of enterprise)

Source: Authors.

- **Large provinces.** About 60% of enterprises reported that it took less than 1 month to renew their TINs in 2019, down from 69% in 2017 ProFIT survey. This is similar to the number of businesses that had to spend over KN3 million to renew their TINs in 2017 and 2019.
- **Medium provinces.** 83.3% enterprises reported spending less than a month to renew their TINs slightly fewer in 2017 ProFIT survey.
- **Small provinces.** The cost and time required to renew TINs fell for the smaller provinces between 2017 and 2019, with 82.1% of companies reporting that the renewal took less than a month, slightly lower than the 85% figure for 2017.

## 4.  Informal Charges

Informal charges remain a major hurdle imposed by the local governments on firms for setting up businesses and running them smoothly (Figure 14). The index includes the share of informal charges to total revenue, acceptability of informal charges, commonality of tax negotiations, necessity of informal charges, and public disclosure of formal charges.

- **Large provinces.** Vientiane Province had the highest score with 66.4 points, while Louangphabang scored only 38.5 largely because of its complicated document procedures, especially requirements for operating licenses, compelling businesses to pay informal charges.
- **Medium provinces.** Salavan and Xiangkhouang were the best performers with a score of slightly above 60 points, followed by Bolikhamxai and Houaphan with about 55 points. Khammouan, Oudomxai, and Xaignabouli failed to reach even 50 points.

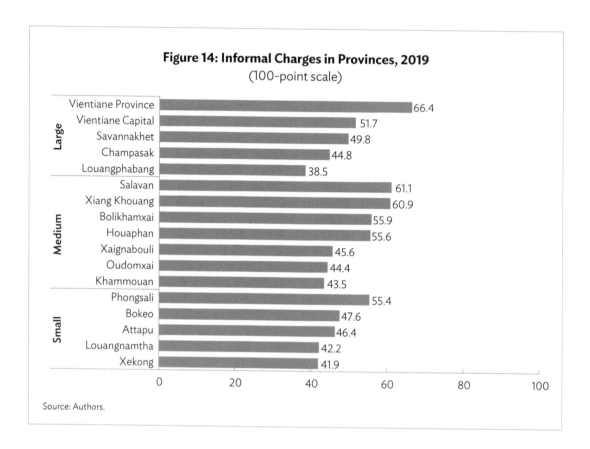

**Figure 14: Informal Charges in Provinces, 2019**
(100-point scale)

Source: Authors.

- **Small provinces.** Most scored lower than 50 points, except for Phongsali, indicating that informal charges are very common in small provinces.

In addition, while progress on reduction of incidence of informal charges is observed between 2017 and 2019, such practices still prevail (Figure 15). Informal practices in business operations are still found to be widespread throughout all provinces and perceived to be part of routine operations, including payment of informal charges and negotiation of taxes (Box 1).

- **Large provinces.** With a 16.6-point gain, Vientiane Province recorded by far the greatest improvement in terms of informal charges paid by enterprises between 2017 and 2019. Vientiane Capital posted only a slight improvement at 1.3 points, as did Louangphabang at 0.7 points, while Champasak improved by 5.2 points and Savannakhet by 6.0 points.
- **Medium provinces.** Salavan improved on its score on informal charges with an increase of 27.5 points, the highest among all provinces as well. In contrast, Oudomxai deteriorated in this category.
- **Small provinces.** Four out of five small provinces recorded declines in informal charges compared to 2017. Only Phongsali improved with an increase of 3.2 points.

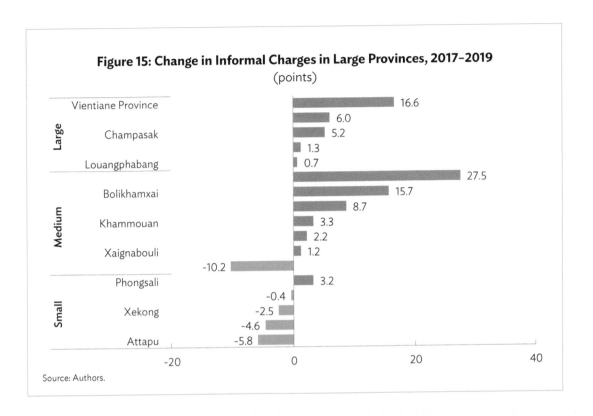

**Figure 15: Change in Informal Charges in Large Provinces, 2017–2019**
(points)

Source: Authors.

## Box 1: Informal Practices in Business Operations in the Lao PDR

All firms are required to report their economic activities to the tax administration, but many firms do not fully report their activities to evade taxation. Such underreporting not only reduces tax collections but also undermines the trust in the tax system and distorts competition among firms. Informal practices in business operations include non-registration of operations, underreporting of enterprise income, payments to officials that are not part of the formal fees, and negotiations of taxes, among others.

The 2019 Provincial Facilitation of Investment and Trade (ProFIT) survey finds that, almost 70% of the respondents, by necessity, paid informal charges for obtaining business registrations, licenses, and permits. Firms also reported having to pay informal charges for accessing government documents as well as to authorities conducting business inspections. Among the respondents who submitted requests to the provincial governments for documents not publicly available, including provincial regulations, instructions, and agreements, 45% paid for informal charges to obtain the documents. Meanwhile, 35% of enterprises paid informal charges to government officials for inspections.

The ProFIT subindex on informal charges uses five indicators: informal charges as share of revenue; and four more indicators representing necessity, commonality, and acceptability of informal charges and public disclosure of formal charges (Table). Findings of the ProFIT survey indicate that informal practices in businesses operations are common and perceived to be part of routine operations, including payment of informal charges. More than two-thirds of enterprises surveyed for this report disclosed that informal payments were necessary to run their operations.

**Informal Charges Indicators**

| Subindex | % | Indicator | Weight (%) |
|---|---|---|---|
| Informal Charges | 100 | Informal charges as a share of revenue | 40 |
| | | Acceptability of informal charges | 15 |
| | | Commonality of tax negotiations | 15 |
| | | Necessity of informal charges | 15 |
| | | Public disclosure of formal charges | 15 |

*continued on next page*

Box 1 *continued*

Tax negotiation practices were found to be widespread throughout all provinces, with nearly 70% of enterprises reporting that it was common to negotiate taxes. Tax negotiation refers to the practice of tax officials and business owners entering negotiations on the amounts of tax payable, rather than basing tax assessments on transparent guidelines and manuals that follow a prescribed method. There are several reasons for this:

(i)    Tax legislation in the country provides room for extensive interpretations of the tax rules and procedures causing opportunities for discretionary decision.
(ii)   The level of education of taxpayers and access to information are limited.
(iii)  Tax officials themselves have limited qualifications or certifications in relevant fields for providing technical assistance to businesses in terms of complying with tax regulation.
(iv)   Tax offices at the provincial level are also responsible for providing information and assistance to taxpayers within their nearest localities, but may not provide systematic and coordinated activities.
(v)    In some cases, tax negotiations are deemed necessary due to lack of double-entry bookkeeping system in firms.

These findings indicate that it is complicated, costly, and time-consuming for businesses to comply with laws, regulations, and procedures in the Lao People's Democratic Republic (Lao PDR). It is therefore an imperative for governments to implement measures that would make registration and the payment of tax easier and more effective, such as through automation and combining registration with other government services, as well as educating businesses on the implications of informal practices for the funding of public services.

Given the inherent problems of accurately estimating the profits of rather small firms in the country, a proposal to replace the profit-based tax with a turnover tax should be seriously considered by the policy makers. The new government headed by a prime minister who is very inclined to involve the private sector in policy making provides a great opportunity for the country to bring about this change in taxation.

Sources: Asian Development Bank. 2021. *Provincial Trade Facilitation Index.* Manila; World Bank. 2019. *Lao PDR Public Expenditure and Financial Accountability Assessment.* Vientiane; Lao Statistics Bureau. 2020. Economic Census.

## 5.  Consistency of Policy Implementation

This subindex tracks business owners' responses to five questions: (i) their perceptions of the advantages of having personal connections, (ii) their opinions on favoritism for state-owned enterprises (SOEs), (iii) consistency of implementation of national rules by the provincial governments, (vi) consistency between provincial and national rules, and (v) interagency coordination in the province to support businesses and provincial rules. Discussions with businesses showed a major cause of inconsistency to be local regulations that are often inconsistent with rules issued by the central government (Figure 16).

- **Large provinces.** Vientiane Province topped the list with a score of 61.1, while Champasak ranked at the bottom with a score of 43.2.
- **Medium provinces.** Salavan topped the list with a score of 64.9, while Bolikhamxai came in at the bottom with a score below 50.
- **Small provinces.** Xekong and Phongsali performed slightly better in this subindex than the other provinces but still posted low scores. Attapu scored the lowest, with only 40.7 points.

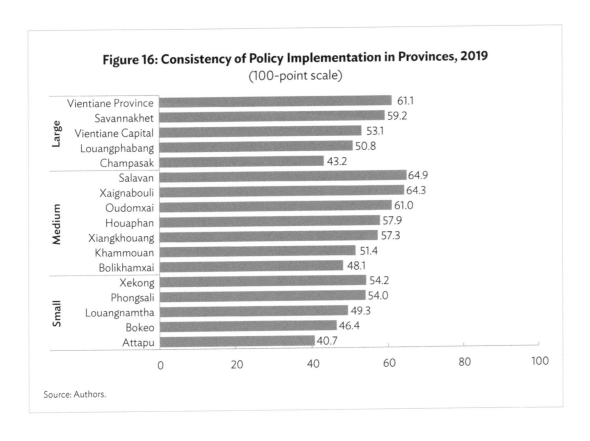

**Figure 16: Consistency of Policy Implementation in Provinces, 2019**
(100-point scale)

Source: Authors.

Policy implementation improved across all provinces, except for Attapu (Figure 17).

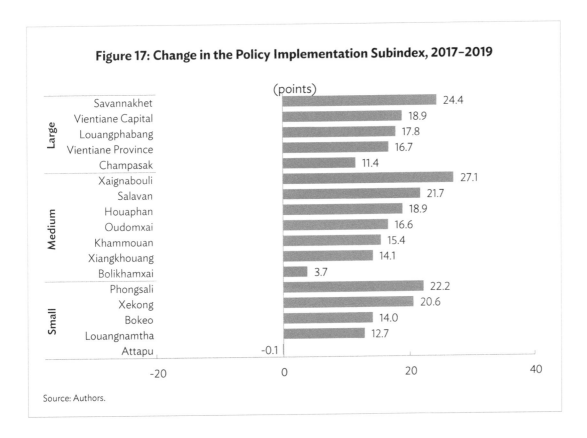

**Figure 17: Change in the Policy Implementation Subindex, 2017–2019**
(points)

Source: Authors.

Provincial governments tend to support SOEs more than private firms (Figure 18). The country has approximately 183 SOEs, mostly established in special economic zones and involved in sectors such as telecommunications, energy, finance, mining, transport, and public utilities. The government has recently embarked upon a program for the restructuring and privatization of SOEs, including increase of private ownership in SOEs through listing on the Lao Securities Exchange. Provincial governments should consider how these reforms can be leveraged to catalyze economic growth in their jurisdictions and to facilitate a more level the playing field for fair competition.

- **Large provinces.** In Savannakhet, 61.5% of respondents perceived that the provincial governments support SOEs more than private firms, as did more than 50% of respondents in Vientiane Capital, Champasak, and Vientiane Province.
- **Medium provinces.** In Xaignabouli, 73.3% of respondents reported that their provincial governments supported SOEs more than private companies, as did 72.7% of respondents in Xiangkhouang.
- **Small provinces.** Nearly two-thirds of respondents in Xekong reported that the provincial government supported SOEs more than private companies, as did in Phongsali (56.7%) and Bokeo (52.5%). Louangnamtha and Attapu were the only provinces in which less than half of responding businesses agreed.

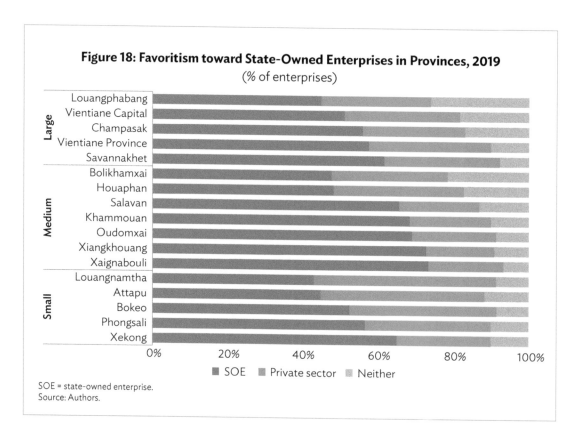

**Figure 18: Favoritism toward State-Owned Enterprises in Provinces, 2019**
(% of enterprises)

SOE = state-owned enterprise.
Source: Authors.

Firms with personal connections to the local government are perceived to receive more favors in terms of contracts, land, and other resources (Figure 19). To reduce nepotism, national and provincial governments need to work together to address this challenge by providing official information online and creating a level playing field across firms, irrespective of their personal connections with the government officials.

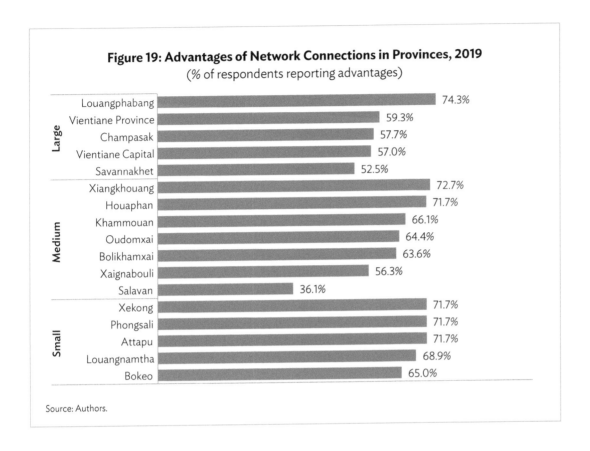

**Figure 19: Advantages of Network Connections in Provinces, 2019**
(% of respondents reporting advantages)

Large
- Louangphabang — 74.3%
- Vientiane Province — 59.3%
- Champasak — 57.7%
- Vientiane Capital — 57.0%
- Savannakhet — 52.5%

Medium
- Xiangkhouang — 72.7%
- Houaphan — 71.7%
- Khammouan — 66.1%
- Oudomxai — 64.4%
- Bolikhamxai — 63.6%
- Xaignabouli — 56.3%
- Salavan — 36.1%

Small
- Xekong — 71.7%
- Phongsali — 71.7%
- Attapu — 71.7%
- Louangnamtha — 68.9%
- Bokeo — 65.0%

Source: Authors.

- **Large provinces.** In Louangphabang, nearly 75% of respondents perceived that they work through personal connections for doing business, while the comparable figures for other provinces were 50%–60%.
- **Medium provinces.** Xiangkhouang had the highest share of respondents, 72.7%, who reported that they had to resort to personal connections with the government to establish and run their businesses, while the scores for the other provinces fell 30%–70%.
- **Small provinces.** In three provinces, 71.7% of respondents had to use their personal connections to run their businesses, although within this average figure there are wide differences across the firms.

The responses were quite varied within provincial groupings on perceptions of the consistency of the implementation of central government policies and regulations at the subnational level (Figure 20).

- **Large provinces.** Over 85% of respondent firms in Savannakhet and Vientiane Province reported consistent implementation of national policies in their provinces.
- **Medium provinces.** Respondents from these provinces had favorable perceptions of central and provincial policy consistency.
- **Small provinces.** These provinces tended to perceive the consistency of implementation of central and subnational policies to be weaker.

Ensuring consistency across national and subnational regulations is critical in improving the business environment. Huge differences are discerned among the provinces in terms of this aspect of business environment (Figure 21).

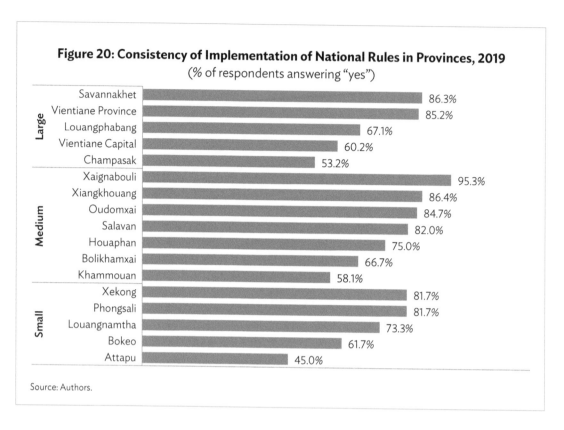

**Figure 20: Consistency of Implementation of National Rules in Provinces, 2019**

(% of respondents answering "yes")

| | | |
|---|---|---|
| **Large** | Savannakhet | 86.3% |
| | Vientiane Province | 85.2% |
| | Louangphabang | 67.1% |
| | Vientiane Capital | 60.2% |
| | Champasak | 53.2% |
| **Medium** | Xaignabouli | 95.3% |
| | Xiangkhouang | 86.4% |
| | Oudomxai | 84.7% |
| | Salavan | 82.0% |
| | Houaphan | 75.0% |
| | Bolikhamxai | 66.7% |
| | Khammouan | 58.1% |
| **Small** | Xekong | 81.7% |
| | Phongsali | 81.7% |
| | Louangnamtha | 73.3% |
| | Bokeo | 61.7% |
| | Attapu | 45.0% |

Source: Authors.

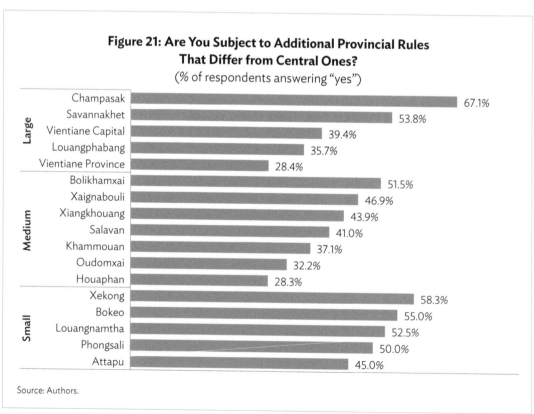

**Figure 21: Are You Subject to Additional Provincial Rules That Differ from Central Ones?**

(% of respondents answering "yes")

| | | |
|---|---|---|
| **Large** | Champasak | 67.1% |
| | Savannakhet | 53.8% |
| | Vientiane Capital | 39.4% |
| | Louangphabang | 35.7% |
| | Vientiane Province | 28.4% |
| **Medium** | Bolikhamxai | 51.5% |
| | Xaignabouli | 46.9% |
| | Xiangkhouang | 43.9% |
| | Salavan | 41.0% |
| | Khammouan | 37.1% |
| | Oudomxai | 32.2% |
| | Houaphan | 28.3% |
| **Small** | Xekong | 58.3% |
| | Bokeo | 55.0% |
| | Louangnamtha | 52.5% |
| | Phongsali | 50.0% |
| | Attapu | 45.0% |

Source: Authors.

- **Large provinces.** More than two-thirds of enterprises in Champasak believed that they are subject to additional provincial rules that are inconsistent with those set by the central government.
- **Medium provinces.** Most of the enterprises in Houaphan perceive provincial rules are consistent with those set by the central government.
- **Small provinces.** More than half of the enterprises in small provinces tended to agree that they are subject to local rules that are different from those from the central ones.

## 6.  Business Friendliness

Business friendliness of the local governments was measured by four indicators: (i) perceived attitude of provincial governments toward private businesses, (ii) provincial government support for private local businesses, (iii) application of new solutions to solve emerging problems, and (iv) awareness in the private sector of PMO 02/2018 (Figure 22).

- **Large provinces.** Scores on business friendliness among large provinces ranged from a little over 50 in Vientiane Province to about 68.8 points in Savannakhet.
- **Medium provinces.** Most of the provinces showed relatively little variation in scores, ranging from 58.4 points in Bolikhamxai to 67.7 points in Xaignabouli.
- **Small provinces.** Attapu, with a score of 62.9 points on business friendliness, topped the list among small provinces, while Louangnamtha was at the bottom of the table.

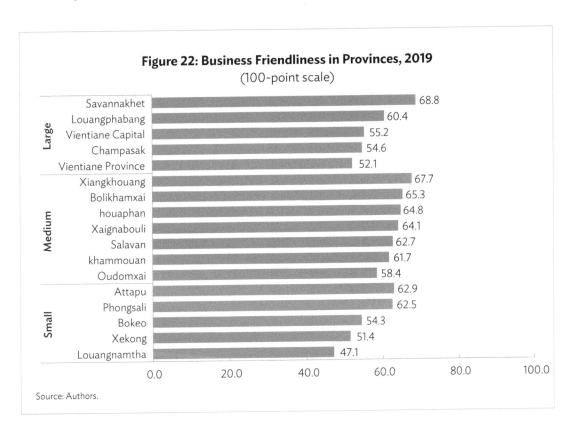

**Figure 22: Business Friendliness in Provinces, 2019**
(100-point scale)

| | Province | Score |
|---|---|---|
| Large | Savannakhet | 68.8 |
| | Louangphabang | 60.4 |
| | Vientiane Capital | 55.2 |
| | Champasak | 54.6 |
| | Vientiane Province | 52.1 |
| Medium | Xiangkhouang | 67.7 |
| | Bolikhamxai | 65.3 |
| | houaphan | 64.8 |
| | Xaignabouli | 64.1 |
| | Salavan | 62.7 |
| | khammouan | 61.7 |
| | Oudomxai | 58.4 |
| Small | Attapu | 62.9 |
| | Phongsali | 62.5 |
| | Bokeo | 54.3 |
| | Xekong | 51.4 |
| | Louangnamtha | 47.1 |

Source: Authors.

The percentage of businesses reporting that provincial governments were willing to assist in the development of the private sector remained quite high (Figure 23).

- **Large provinces.** 87.5% respondents in Savannakhet perceived that their provincial governments had a positive attitude toward the private sector, while Champasak was at the bottom of list with a score of only 55.1%.
- **Medium provinces.** More than 70% of respondents thought their provincial government had a positive attitude toward the private sector and would apply fresh solutions to resolve emerging problems for the businesses.
- **Small provinces.** Over 70% of respondents in Phongsali, Xekong, Louangnamtha, and Attapu said their provincial governments had a positive attitude toward the private sector and were willing to apply innovative solutions to resolve challenges facing private businesses, while fewer than 60% of respondents in Bokeo agreed.

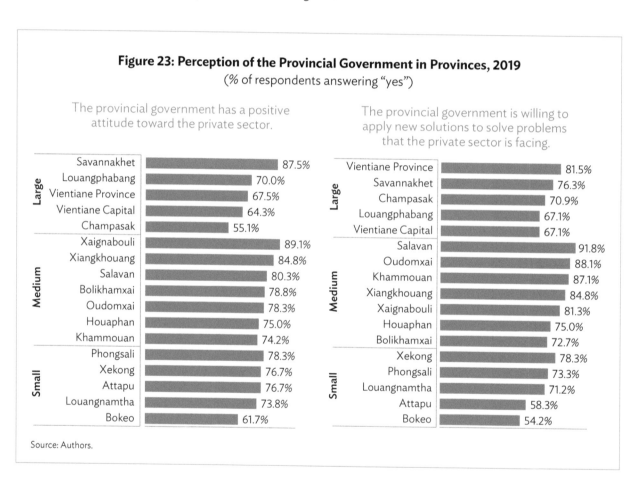

**Figure 23: Perception of the Provincial Government in Provinces, 2019**
(% of respondents answering "yes")

The provincial government has a positive attitude toward the private sector.

| | Province | % |
|---|---|---|
| Large | Savannakhet | 87.5% |
| | Louangphabang | 70.0% |
| | Vientiane Province | 67.5% |
| | Vientiane Capital | 64.3% |
| | Champasak | 55.1% |
| Medium | Xaignabouli | 89.1% |
| | Xiangkhouang | 84.8% |
| | Salavan | 80.3% |
| | Bolikhamxai | 78.8% |
| | Oudomxai | 78.3% |
| | Houaphan | 75.0% |
| | Khammouan | 74.2% |
| Small | Phongsali | 78.3% |
| | Xekong | 76.7% |
| | Attapu | 76.7% |
| | Louangnamtha | 73.8% |
| | Bokeo | 61.7% |

The provincial government is willing to apply new solutions to solve problems that the private sector is facing.

| | Province | % |
|---|---|---|
| Large | Vientiane Province | 81.5% |
| | Savannakhet | 76.3% |
| | Champasak | 70.9% |
| | Louangphabang | 67.1% |
| | Vientiane Capital | 67.1% |
| Medium | Salavan | 91.8% |
| | Oudomxai | 88.1% |
| | Khammouan | 87.1% |
| | Xiangkhouang | 84.8% |
| | Xaignabouli | 81.3% |
| | Houaphan | 75.0% |
| | Bolikhamxai | 72.7% |
| Small | Xekong | 78.3% |
| | Phongsali | 73.3% |
| | Louangnamtha | 71.2% |
| | Attapu | 58.3% |
| | Bokeo | 54.2% |

Source: Authors.

# Chapter 4

Selected Policy Issues

## A. Enterprise Structure in the Lao PDR

The Lao PDR Bureau of Statistics has conducted three economic census surveys over 15 years—in 2006, 2013, and 2020. The economic census provides important information on the state of enterprises in the country, such as their activities by sector, employment, enterprise size, revenues and expenditures, finance, and compliance with various regulatory requirements. These census surveys show that enterprise growth has been limited over the last 15 years, both in terms of the total number of enterprises and the overall structure of enterprises by size (Table 8).

**Table 8: Selected Enterprise Indicators, 2006–2020**

(%)

| Variable | 2006 | 2013 | 2020 |
|---|---|---|---|
| **Business registration** | | | |
| - Yes | 40.0 | 34.9 | 30.4 |
| - No | 60.0 | 65.1 | 69.6 |
| **Tax identification number** | | | |
| - Yes | 8.0 | 14.8 | 12.9 |
| - No | 92.0 | 85.2 | 87.1 |
| **Enterprise size** | | | |
| - Micro | 93.5 | 86.0 | 94.2 |
| - Small | 4.2 | 9.2 | 4.9 |
| - Medium | 2.2 | 5.0 | 0.7 |
| - Large | 0.2 | 0.2 | 0.7 |

Note: The definition for the enterprise size in 2020 is different following Prime Minister's Decree No. 25 dated 16 January 2017 on the categories of small and medium-sized enterprises.
Source: Lao Statistics Bureau. Economic Census. Selected years.

Micro- and small enterprises dominate the business structure of the economy. In 2020, microenterprises accounted for 94.2% of all enterprises, followed by small enterprises at 4.9%, medium-sized enterprises at 0.7%, and large enterprises at 0.2%. In terms of employment, most enterprises have five or less employees (90.6%), while enterprises with more than 50 employees account for only 0.4% of enterprises (Figure 24). In terms of the education level of the enterprise owners, two-thirds of them have at best have a high school degree.

Informality is also high, particularly among micro and small enterprises. In 2020, only 30.4% of enterprises reported that they had registered their business, a decline from 34.9% in 2013 and 40.0% in 2006. The proportion of enterprises that had TINs improved marginally, from 8.0% in 2006 to 12.9% in 2020. However, the overall share of enterprises with TINs remains low (Figure 25). Meanwhile, the burden of compliance with business regulations is comparatively higher for smaller enterprises, due to the fixed components of the cost and the time required for obtaining registration, licenses, and permits for starting a business. Firms that are fully registered reported high levels of scrutiny by authorities, working as a disincentive for enterprises to formalize by registering with the authorities.

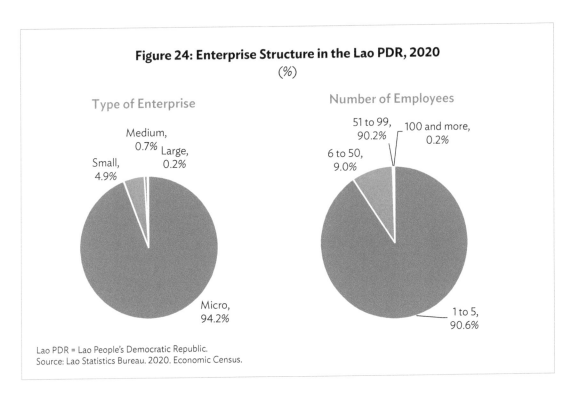

**Figure 24: Enterprise Structure in the Lao PDR, 2020**
(%)

Type of Enterprise

Medium, 0.7% Large, 0.2%
Small, 4.9%
Micro, 94.2%

Number of Employees

51 to 99, 90.2% 100 and more, 0.2%
6 to 50, 9.0%
1 to 5, 90.6%

Lao PDR = Lao People's Democratic Republic.
Source: Lao Statistics Bureau. 2020. Economic Census.

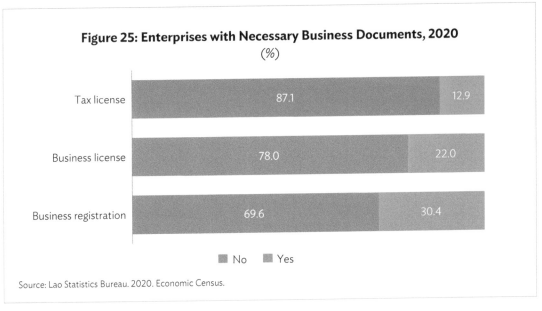

**Figure 25: Enterprises with Necessary Business Documents, 2020**
(%)

| | No | Yes |
|---|---|---|
| Tax license | 87.1 | 12.9 |
| Business license | 78.0 | 22.0 |
| Business registration | 69.6 | 30.4 |

Source: Lao Statistics Bureau. 2020. Economic Census.

Usage of formal finance, modern accounting methods, and ICT is quite limited among most enterprises. Only 3.3% of enterprises follow general accounting systems and 0.5% apply double-entry accounting, with 96.4% of enterprises not practicing any kind of accounting at all. Lack of reliable accounting systems makes it difficult to understand and evaluate the balance sheets and the income and expenditures of enterprises. That, in turn, hinders an accurate estimate of the tax liabilities of enterprises. Only 6.6% of enterprises reported that they used ICT tools in running their business in 2020 and only 9.6% reported that they had obtained a loan from formal financial institutions, such as a bank, in the last 3 years. Low utilization of credit, technology, and financial management tools point to weak incentives for enterprises to grow.

When asked about perceived constraints facing their enterprise, businesses reported market access as one of the biggest issues, followed by the country's business environment. Moreover, compliance with business regulations has not improved substantially over time. It is therefore likely that the complex regulatory environment for businesses is a binding constraint on enterprise growth and is potentially a key factor underlying limited enterprise growth over the last 15 years. This situation thus requires urgent attention from policy makers, as the absence of effective reforms to spur enterprise growth entails a risk for the country's growth and development outlook.

## B.  Impact of PMO 02/2018 on Business Registration

The passage of PMO 02/2018 is intended to reduce the cost and time required to register a new business (Figure 26). Survey data collected for this report shows that enterprises established in 2019 that were registered under PMO 02/2018 processes paid on average KN1.7 million to register their business, while companies established under previous procedures spent KN2.6 million. However, formal fees reported in laws are only KN590,000, therefore fees paid are still more than double the officially required payments. This suggests that informal payments, such as expediting fees, play a large role in securing regulatory compliance.

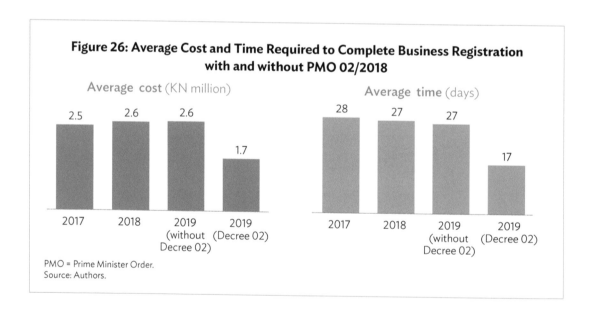

**Figure 26: Average Cost and Time Required to Complete Business Registration with and without PMO 02/2018**

PMO = Prime Minister Order.
Source: Authors.

On a positive note, with PMO 02/2018, the average time required to complete the registration process shortened from 27 days in 2017 to 17 days in 2019. However, this is higher than the mandated 10 days for obtaining enterprise registration certificate in accordance with MOIC Decree No.0023 on Decision on Enterprise Registration, dated 9 January 2019 (Box 2). Such inconsistent application of government regulations at the subnational level has implications for general business sentiment and may explain why enterprises reported that they perceived the regulatory environment to be one of the most significant constraints that they face in doing business, as reported in the 2020 economic census.

## Box 2: Recent Reforms to Procedures for Starting a Business

Based on recent reforms to procedures for starting a business (Figure), an enterprise registration certificate (ERC) shall take no more than 10 working days. This is in accordance with the Ministry of Industry and Commerce Decree No.0023 on Decision on Enterprise Registration, dated 9 January 2019. The securing of company seal and its approval will take no more than 5 working days for issuance, as per the Ministry of Public Security Decision No. 1784 dated 2 October 2018 regarding Management and Production of Seal. A social security registration certificate is to be approved within 2 working days according to the Ministry of Labor and Social Affairs Instruction No.1206 dated 23 April 2019. The new process was launched in February 2019 for all provinces. Some businesses are required to apply for a business operating license with relevant sector agencies. If business activities are classified as conditioned, controlled, or concession as defined in Decree No.03/PM dated 10 January 2019 on Endorsement of List of Controlled and Concession Activities, investors are given 90 days after the issuance of the ERC to secure the relevant business operation license and provide the relevant enterprise registration office with an official copy.

### Figure: Procedures for Starting a Business in the Lao PDR

Lao PDR = Lao People's Democratic Republic.
Source: National Enterprise Database. http://www.ned.moic.gov.la/index.php/en/.

The share of firms reporting having to pay informal charges for registration declined between 2017 and 2019 (Figure 27). This implies that PMO 02/2018 supported reductions in the cost and time required for business registration. However, the incidence of informal payments during business registration remained largely unchanged, leaving most business owners continuing to pay informal charges to establish their businesses. Despite regulatory reforms that have made it easier to do business, enterprises and authorities still have the discretion to negotiate informal charges.

**Figure 27: Informal Payments during Business Registration, 2017–2019**
(% of firms paying informal charges)

Source: Authors.

Most companies reported that they were not yet aware of PMO 02/2018. Only 22% of the respondents were aware of PMO 02/2018 (Figure 28). Further efforts are therefore needed to disseminate PMO 02/2018, particularly considering business' concerns on low transparency and poor access to information. In addition, improvements in the compliance with regulatory requirements are needed through a consistent application and enforcement of business regulations. Improvements are needed in human resources, including the governments' capacity for enforcement of the regulatory framework at the subnational level.

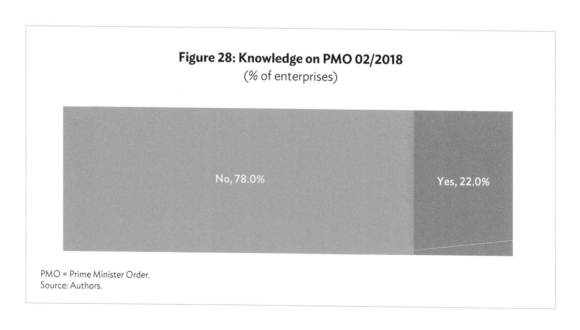

**Figure 28: Knowledge on PMO 02/2018**
(% of enterprises)

PMO = Prime Minister Order.
Source: Authors.

## C. Excessive Cost Burden on Private Businesses

Although PMO 02/2018 provided a set of critical reforms, enterprises in the country remain disadvantaged by lack of transparency, high cost of excessive registration, licensing, and permit requirements, and practice of informal payments (Figure 29). Even after the passage of PMO 02/2018, more than two-thirds of companies in the country reported that they had to pay informal charges to obtain operating licenses from local governments once they registered their businesses. Even though the value of informal payments may have reduced, the overall prevalence of these informal practices point to the need for strengthening local governance to reduce rent-seeking opportunities.

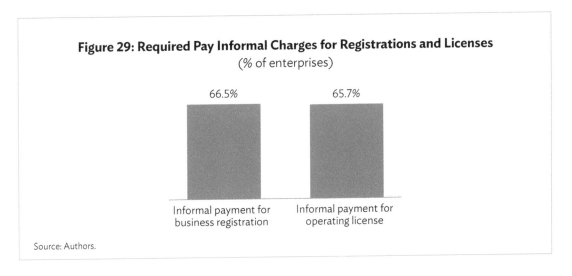

**Figure 29: Required Pay Informal Charges for Registrations and Licenses**
(% of enterprises)

66.5%          65.7%

Informal payment for          Informal payment for
business registration          operating license

Source: Authors.

Available evidence seems to point to large differences across the government ministries that businesses have to deal with in obtaining business operating licenses (Figure 30).

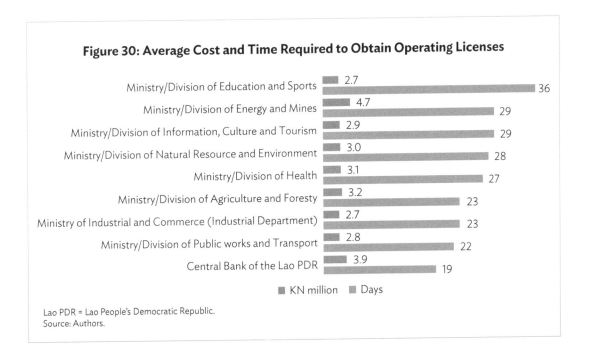

**Figure 30: Average Cost and Time Required to Obtain Operating Licenses**

| | KN million | Days |
|---|---|---|
| Ministry/Division of Education and Sports | 2.7 | 36 |
| Ministry/Division of Energy and Mines | 4.7 | 29 |
| Ministry/Division of Information, Culture and Tourism | 2.9 | 29 |
| Ministry/Division of Natural Resource and Environment | 3.0 | 28 |
| Ministry/Division of Health | 3.1 | 27 |
| Ministry/Division of Agriculture and Foresty | 3.2 | 23 |
| Ministry of Industrial and Commerce (Industrial Department) | 2.7 | 23 |
| Ministry/Division of Public works and Transport | 2.8 | 22 |
| Central Bank of the Lao PDR | 3.9 | 19 |

Lao PDR = Lao People's Democratic Republic.
Source: Authors.

The average cost of completing business registration in 2019 was KN1.9 million, taking on average of 19 days. The average time required for a firm to start its business with operating licenses in 2018 and 2019 was 32 days, and the cost about KN5 million, on the average (Figure 31). Operating licenses must be renewed every year, with the process taking an average of 17 days and costing KN2.1 million a year. In addition to renewing their operating licenses, companies must renew their TINs every year, and this takes an average of 16 days and costs about KN2 million. The costs of renewing TINs and operating licenses are often higher than the cost of initial business registration.

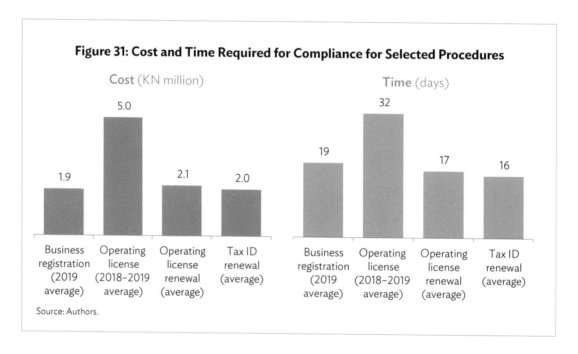

**Figure 31: Cost and Time Required for Compliance for Selected Procedures**

Source: Authors.

Many businesses in the country must pay informal charges to conduct their business operations. On average, these informal charges account for 5.6% of an enterprise's revenue. More than two-thirds of the firms reported that informal payments were forced upon them to ensure their business operations, and a similar proportion of firms said that it was common to negotiate the amount of taxes they paid to the local governments (Figure 32).

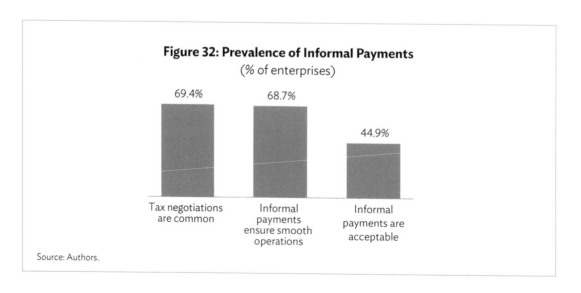

**Figure 32: Prevalence of Informal Payments**
(% of enterprises)

Source: Authors.

This causes a formidable administrative barrier to formal market entry in terms of the high cost and time required to obtain company registration and operating licenses, and the requirement that TINs and operation licenses be renewed annually. Only about 45% of respondents said this was acceptable, the remaining firms find it unacceptable but have no choice to avoid them.

The Lao PDR is the only country in Southeast Asia requiring firms to renew their TINs and business operating licenses every year. Regional and international comparative analysis that follow standardized methodologies also provide useful information for benchmarking how the Lao PDR compares with its neighbors (Box 3).

### Box 3: World Bank Assessments of the Business Environment

The World Bank monitors and reports on 12 aspects of business regulation globally via an international survey conducted with experts. For the Lao People's Democratic Republic (Lao PDR), the World Bank surveys 50 professional groups and private sector experts based in Vientiane Capital. The survey, published with a 1-year time lag, measures indicators on regulations for starting a business, among others, based on a review of laws and regulations, as well as implementation of these procedures, by legal experts. In this sense, the survey captures information on reform implementation related to bureaucracy efficiency. The World Bank survey identifies nine procedures required to start a business in the Lao PDR and reported that it took 173 days to complete these procedures in 2020. The nine procedures are: (i) Enterprise Registration Certificate (ERC)–60 to 90 days ; (ii) Register the Articles of Association–7 days; (iii) Apply for Tax Registration Certificate–30 days; (iv) Attend a tax orientation meeting and obtain Tax Identification Number (TIN)–30 days; (v) Carve a company seal–14 days; (vi) Register company seal at the department of public security–up to 14 days; (vii) Obtain Approval of Content on the Company Signage–up to 14 days; (viii) Register the workers for social security–7 days; and (ix) Register for Value-Added Tax–21 days.

In contrast, the Provincial Facilitation of Investment and Trade (ProFIT) Index is based on a survey of 1,357 enterprise owners across 17 provinces on six subindexes for providing information on the business environment at the subnational level. ProFIT has different scope, with only three procedures assessed, with these requiring 60 days to complete on average. The three procedures are (i) ERC–28 days on average; (ii) TIN–included under ERC processes; (iii) Business operating license–32 days on average. The ProFIT survey results include efficiency gains outlined in the latest government reforms that streamline procedures in starting a business, such as issues of tax identification numbers with the ERC.

Sources: Asian Development Bank. 2022. Provincial Trade Facilitation Index. Manila; World Bank. 2021. *Country Economic Memorandum.* Vientiane.

A comprehensive regulatory reform program is indeed needed in the Lao PDR to reduce the number of days to obtain registrations, licenses, and permits by simplifying regulations and administrative procedures, and improving the transparency of implementation of business policies at the subnational level. In particular, the government should enable companies to start doing businesses immediately after completing their business registration. A program of introducing e-business registration can help reduce the cost and time required for business registration, as has been done by the neighboring country Cambodia (Box 4).

Such a regulatory reform agenda should aim at reducing the cost and time required for enterprises to obtain the necessary compliance documents, curtailing informal payments, and improving transparency. The government should enact such a reform agenda as soon as possible to produce tangible results over the medium term, as other neighboring countries in the region have done (Box 5).

## Box 4: Cambodia Online Business Registration System

The Government of Cambodia launched its new single portal online business registration system on 15 June 2020. It allows investors to register their business and taxes on one platform, thus reducing unnecessary procedures. Further, all fees can be paid online through various e-payment options. The aim is to approve applications within 8 working days.

Six government bodies are integrated into this single portal online business registration system: the Ministry of Interior, Ministry of Economy and Finance, Ministry of Commerce, Ministry of Labor and Vocational Training, General Department of Taxation, and Council for the Development of Cambodia. It is expected that by using this system investors avoid delays and informal charges. The government aims to expand the system to all ministries and institutions, meaning all licenses and certificates will be issued digitally going forward.

Source: Association of Southeast Asian Nations (ASEAN) Briefing. 2020. *Cambodia Launches New Online Business Registration System*. https://www.aseanbriefing.com/news/cambodia-launches-new-online-business-registration-system/.

## Box 5: Regulatory Reform in Viet Nam

Lack of transparency in business operations was a major problem in Viet Nam, but the nation is now working to address this problem. Viet Nam has met all transparency requirements published by the World Trade Organization, including making all laws and regulations available online for public comment at least 60 days before they are due to go into effect. Issuing agencies are required to report major comments to policy makers for consideration in revising draft regulations. Each province, ministry, and court maintains official public websites that feature regulations in both draft and final version.

The Prime Minister of Viet Nam set up a new unit in 2011 called the Administrative Procedure Control Agency (APCA), which was tasked with leading the reform of administrative procedures and regulations and with developing e-government. The agency is advised by an advisory committee on administrative procedure reform made up of foreign and local business groups. APCA now requires a list of all administrative procedures and official fees to be published online and at the physical public offices where public services are delivered.

APCA launched a massive regulatory reform initiative in 2012 to streamline thousands of regulations and procedures. More recently, major business leaders formed the Private Sector Development Committee, with endorsement from the Prime Minister, and pooled their resources to support a full-time secretariat to work with the Office of the Government on regulatory reform. In 2018, the Committee and the APCA launched the Administrative Procedure Compliance Index, which ranked ministries and agencies by the cost of compliance with their procedures, based on feedback from business users. The Office of the Government set up an online public services portal in February 2020 that integrates all administrative procedures, with e-payment, e-signature, and tracking features. This portal enabled companies and citizens to make online transactions during the coronavirus disease (COVID-19) outbreak, and citizens and companies could submit their feedback and suggestions for improving the portal directly to the Office of the Government.

Source: Authors.

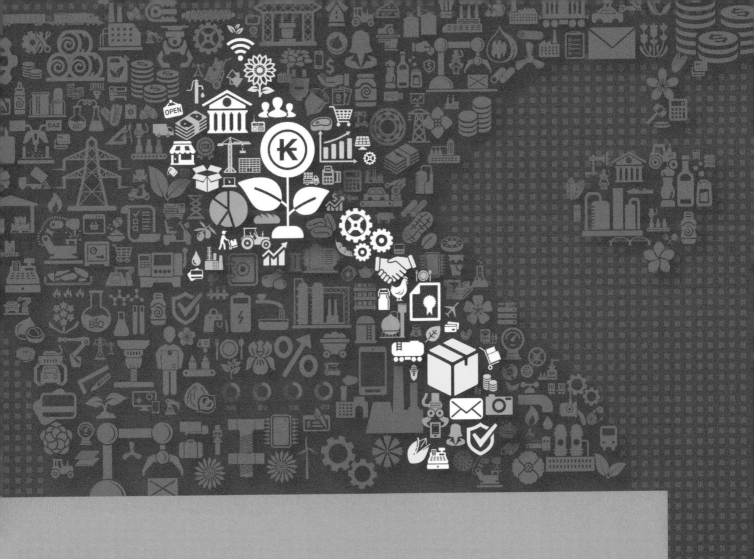

# Chapter 5

## Policy Options

The ProFIT survey, the second in its edition, presents the views of 1,357 business enterprises in 17 provinces across the Lao PDR on subnational governance indicators for the domestic business environment. The overall business environment improved across all provinces as most provinces recorded higher scores in the second edition when compared to the first, pointing to some improvements in local business conditions.

Among the provinces, Vientiane Province recorded the highest score on the ProFIT index, outperforming other provinces in terms of reducing regulatory burden and informal charges. However, Savannakhet Province recorded the largest improvement between 2017 and 2019. The province improved in all areas of business environment, particularly on the consistency of policy implementation and lowering regulatory burden. Despite these improvements, there is considerable scope for simplifying procedures and providing incentives for inducing much more investment from the private sector. This underscores the need for a major simplification of the country's business environment, strengthening the competencies of the civil service, and equally importantly, making the civil service more bsuiness-friendly.

Despite the overall improvement in the second edition of ProFIT index, progress has been lethargic in terms of progress on transparency and access to information (TAI), business friendliness, and informal charges. In 2019, 11 out of 17 provinces had websites, and this had reduced to 7 at the time of publication of this report. But the effectiveness of dissemination of new regulations, as well as the quality of communication infrastructure and systems for supporting the dissemination was still limited. The ProFIT 2019 survey also confirms that the government has commenced implementation of the reform program per PMO 02/2018, with several survey respondents reporting reduced cost and time required to start a business after the promulgation of the reform program.

Excessive regulatory requirements and payments of informal charges at the local government levels still pose a key challenge to most businesses. More than 70% of enterprises in the country had to pay informal charges to local governments to ensure that they obtain registration, licenses, and permits to operate. A considerable amount of tax revenues is lost due to these practices, suggesting a need to revisit policies that govern the business environment with a view to improving the attractiveness of both domestic and foreign investments into the country. Diligence in reform implementation is required to improve the ease of enterprise registration across all provinces for creating more formal sector jobs and supporting the country in achieving the many objectives of the Ninth National Socio-Economic Development Plan as well as to help the country to achieve many of the goals set out in the Agenda 2030 on Sustainable Development.

Recent policy measures aimed at consolidating the regulatory requirements on businesses have led to an overall improvement in business environment across most provinces the country. However, progress in terms of the transparency of provincial rules and regulations has been lackluster, leaving considerable scope for further improvements to make the business environment more business friendly. Informal business practices were still pervasive, with adverse implications for enterprise growth and government revenue collections. The findings of the report indicate that firms in the Lao PDR remain disadvantaged due to excessive regulatory requirements and continued informal practices, especially compared to the neighboring countries such as Cambodia and Viet Nam. More than two-thirds of enterprises in the country reported that they had to pay informal charges to local government officials for registering their businesses, obtaining licenses, and permits. Tax negotiation practices between enterprises and local government officials are widespread across all provincial-level governments. A transformative business environment reform agenda, implemented with efficiency and integrity, is needed to bolster business sentiment to drive a strong post COVID-19 recovery.

Key policy options that both subnational governments and the central government should seriously consider going forward are summarized below, particularly concerning consolidation of requirements to spur formalization, improving transparency, and improving the quality of policy implementation.

## Consolidate Regulatory Requirements to Incentivize Business Formalization

1.  **E-business registration consolidation.** Implementation of consolidated online business registration processes should be expedited. One key recommendation in PMO 02/2018 was to allow businesses to register online. Cambodia, and Viet Nam have recently moved toward online business registration, which has significantly reduced the cost and time required for business operations in those countries. Businesses in the Lao PDR are still required to register offline both nationally and provincially and are also required to coordinate with various sector agencies, which means high transaction costs including the financial cost as well as the cost of delays. A program of e-business registration should place online the information about regulations and the applications firms must complete before starting their operations. However, since more than 95% of the first covered in this report are small and micro-sized, it remains to be seen if they could be sufficiently trained to grasp the tools of the new information technology. A program of training those firms in using information technology tools—funded by the government or jointly funded by the government and the enterprises—could be of great help in firms embracing the information technology tools.

2.  **Reform licensing and inspection.** At present, local governments in the country require businesses comply with the regulatory framework even before they start operations. International experience shows that, except for high-risk activities, it is preferable to control and mitigate risks during business operations when the processes and practices of businesses are fully functioning. Rules and standards are made explicit at the start-up stage and then monitored thorough inspections during operations and not before. This allows a better assessment of how a business operates. After the start-up of operations, inspections have a higher probability of ensuring compliance with the law, rules, and standards, as opposed to inspections conducted before a business starts its operations. In addition to these reforms in licensing and inspection, there is considerable merit in simplifying the cumbersome bankruptcy procedures in the country. For the firms to flourish, a well-functioning exit strategy through reasonable bankruptcy procedures is as important as the reforms to simplify procedures to enable firms to register their business.

3.  **Introduce a risk-based licensing regime.** Reform requirements for issuance of business operating license following systematic use of a "risk-based approach" licensing regime, which encourages licensing authorities to use business operating licenses as a mitigation tool, rather than default tool, to address significant risks that a business activity can generate to the health, safety, and security of citizens, consumers, other businesses, and the environment. In other words, business operating license requirements on sectors and activities should be based on evidence-based assessments that conclude that a high probability and a significant magnitude of the harm can occur by the starting of the business activity. Actioning such an approach will further consolidate requirements on businesses for complying with regulations.

## Improve Transparency and Access to Information at Central and Provincial Levels

4. **Improving access to information on regulations.** The government, at both central and subnational levels, should make publicly available a consistent and complete inventory of regulatory requirements. This includes the step-by-step procedures to start a business and comply with government regulations, such as registration, licensing, inspection, and taxation. Often, authorities do not make this information available to businesses in a user-friendly way, forcing businesses to make several visits to government offices to obtain such information. The authorities could resolve this issue by keeping an online inventory of requirements and updating that information regularly at the central level and ensure that this repository is linked with subnational government websites.

5. **Transparency through minimum standards for provincial websites.** E-government cannot be implemented unless provinces have official websites that are easily accessible for existing businesses and potential investors, domestic or foreign. However, provincial websites across the country vary substantially in their quality and in their completeness, with serious implications for TAI for enterprises. A provincial website should at the minimum feature provincial budgets, public procurement opportunities, socioeconomic development plans, land-use plans, lists of formal fees, rules and regulations, public notices of draft local rules for the public to provide suggestions and comments, and forms and administrative procedures. Most of the population in the Lao PDR is now covered by the mobile network with access to the internet, indicating that the high level of digital connectivity would support efficient distribution of information via official government websites to a large portion of the population.

6. **Consolidation of government services to online platforms.** Central and provincial governments need to consider how best could they comprehensively deploy their services online to minimize face-to-face interaction. Tax transactions and customs payments should move online as quickly as possible to reduce compliance costs and curtail opportunities for rent-seeking. Other services involving businesses, such as social security or insurance programs, could be digitally connected with business registration and taxation platforms.

## Quality of Policy Formulation and Implementation at Central and Provincial Levels

7. **Public–private dialogues.** It is essential that governments at all levels engage with the private sector through a collaboration to identify issues, future potential, and solutions closely and systematically. The collaboration should have a strong technical focus on analyzing impediments to businesses, as well as understanding current and future regional and global market needs, while avoiding overregulation and subsidies. The annual Lao Business Forum is an example of best practice in such dialogues that can be replicated at sector and subnational levels. Local government leaders play a critical role in promoting local private sector development. Subnational governments should therefore consider establishing taskforces with the mandate of building up such public–private dialogues.

8. **Empowering the interministerial task force on business environment reform.** Raise the profile and empower the recently appointed interministerial task force to undertake a transformative reform agenda to enable the private sector to take a significant role in the country's post-pandemic recovery. This includes support for prioritization and sequencing of reforms and strengthening the ability of the task force to coordinate the among the ministries and subnational governments.

9. **Talent management and human capital development for better governance.** Enhance the capacity of central and subnational government officials to improve the regulatory environment for businesses by investing in information systems and data management. Online capacity-building training methods as well as related information and technology systems need to be upgraded. Subscribing to services, such as those offered under Microsoft Office 365 including SharePoint and Outlook, could offer quick wins for modernizing services and upgrading operations. Digital literacy has become an important competence, along with skills in strategy and decision-making. Investment in these areas would contribute to improvements in governance and a strengthening of effectiveness of decision-making needed for improving the business environment.

This report notes progress in the procedures and implementation of policy reforms aimed at reducing the hurdles to business development and diversification at the subnational level in the country. Yet, there is substantial scope for further improvement, as has been recognized by the government in its Ninth National Socio-Economic Development Plan for 2021–2025. The Lao PDR's economy and business community were hit hard by the COVID-19 pandemic. Overcoming the challenges posed by COVID-19 will require private sector as well as governments at all levels to change their practices. Implementation and execution of critical reforms to reduce the cost and risk of doing business is essential for attracting new investments to boost economic recovery. The ProFIT index and its subcomponents provide a tool to enhance dialogue between private sector and the local governments in the country.

The report sheds some important light on the improvements that took place in 2019 because of various government initiatives and points to some of the implementation challenges. Such an assessment of subnational government performance is useful to monitor regulatory implementation on the ground, as well as to drive reform efforts outside of the central government and Vientiane Capital. This type of assessment will become more important going forward, following the government's recent emphasis on decentralization of approval authority and implementation responsibilities to provincial governments, particularly concerning tax policy administration.

That said, the report should end with a word of caution. While subnational governments can always try to make the business environment investor-friendly, they are bound to operate within the rules set by the central government. A large part of the time and cost burden on businesses in the Lao PDR stems from rules administered by central government agencies, such as the requirement to renew TIN numbers and operating licenses annually, in addition to complex procedures for setting up companies. This continues to set the limits on the reforms and business liberalization measures that subnational governments can undertake.

# Appendix

## ProFIT Questionnaire 2019

**Provincial Facilitation of Investment and Trade Index (ProFIT Index 2019)**

Lao National Chamber of Commerce and Industry (LNCCI) thanks you for joining us in this survey. The survey gives you a unique opportunity to rate the local business environment and improve the business environment for your company. The LNCCI warrants that all information gathered shall be kept in strict confidence and your business will not be impacted.

1. Your name: _____     2. Position: _____

3. Mobile phone: _____     4. Email: _____

5. Your company business registration No: _____

6. Have you ever participated in assessment on provincial facilitation of investment and trade organized by LNCCI in 2017?

1 ☐ Yes          0 ☐ No

### A. General information about your enterprise

A1. Company name and address: _____

A2. When is your company is established? _____

A3. Your province *

| code | province | code | province |
|------|----------|------|----------|
| 1 | Phongsali | 9 | Vientiane |
| 2 | Louangnamtha | 10 | Vientiane Capital |
| 3 | Oudomxai | 11 | Bolikhamxai |
| 4 | Bokeo | 12 | Khammouan |
| 5 | Louangphabang | 13 | Savannakhet |
| 6 | Houaphan | 14 | Salavan |
| 7 | Xaignabouli | 15 | Xekong |
| 8 | Xiangkhouang | 16 | Champasak |
| | | 17 | Attapu |

A4. Gender of your managing director

0 ☐ Female          1 ☐ Male

A5. Do woman shareholders/owners have equal or more than 30% ownership

1 ☐ Yes          0 ☐ No

A6. Which sector does your company operate in?

1 ☐ Production          2 ☐ Services          3 ☐ Manufacturing

4 ☐ Construction          5 ☐ Agriculture, forestry, fisheries

6 ☐ Trading, whole, sales and retailing

7 ☐ Other:

A7. What are your main products/services? _____

A8. Type of company

1 ☐ Ordinary partnership          2 ☐ Limited liability partnership

3 ☐ Public company          4 ☐ Limited company

A9. Number of full-time workers? _____ people

A10. Did you expand your business in 2018?

1 ☐ Yes          0 ☐ No

A11. Do you plan to expand your business in 2019 and 2020?

1 ☐ Yes          0 ☐ No

## B. Starting a business

B1. How did you obtain your business registration, operating license and permits to start your business?

1 ☐ Filed by myself or by my staff

0 ☐ Use external services (law, consulting firm, consultant)

B2. How did your company receive business license?

1 ☐ Receive business license the same time with tax identification number

2 ☐ Receive business license did not the same time with tax identification number

3 ☐ Other (specify) _____

B2.1 How many days did it take to complete your company registration (i.e., from submission of all the documents until receipt of company seal and registration certificate)
Total time spent (official working day) _____ days

B2.2 How much did you spend on obtaining business registration including all formal and informal charges (in Million LAK) _____

B.2.3. Do you think companies in your sector will have to pay informal charges to obtain the business registration?

1 ☐ Yes                    0 ☐ No.

B3. Did you have to obtain an operating license and other permits to start your business

1 ☐ Yes (answer 3.1.1-3.3.5)   0 ☐ No (answer B4)

B3.1 Please let us know the name of the operating license and permit and the agencies that issues them, day took for obtain the license, and cost to obtain the license and permit?

| No. 1 | Name of licensee | Time (days) | Cost (Million KIP) |
|---|---|---|---|
| B.3.1.1 | | | |
| B3.1.2 | | | |
| B3.1.3 | | | |

B3.2 Do you think companies in your sector will have to pay informal charges to obtain the following licenses and permits?

1 ☐ Yes (answer B3.2.1)        0 ☐ No (answer B4)

B3.2.1 If yes, please specify the name of the licenses and permits

No. 1 _____

No. 2 _____

No. 3 _____

B4. Please tell us your experience in completing the following procedures for business registration.

| Business establishment | The most difficult | Least difficulty | Not difficulty at all | Don't know |
|---|---|---|---|---|
| B4.1 Business license | 3 | 2 | 1 | 9 |
| B4.2 Tax certificate | 3 | 2 | 1 | 9 |
| B4.3 Company seal | 3 | 2 | 1 | 9 |
| B4.4 Operating license | 3 | 2 | 1 | 9 |
| B4.5 Amending business license | 3 | 2 | 1 | 9 |
| B4.6 Others (specify) _____ | 3 | 2 | 1 | 9 |

## C. Transparency And Access To Information

C1. Please let us know whether the below documents are published by the local government or accessible by anybody

| Document | Yes | No | Don't know |
|---|---|---|---|
| C11 Provincial budget | 1 ☐ | 2 ☐ | 9 ☐ |
| C12 Provincial Socio-economic development plan | 1 ☐ | 2 ☐ | 9 ☐ |
| C13 Provincial regulations, instruction, and agreement | 1 ☐ | 2 ☐ | 9 ☐ |
| C14 Provincial investment budget for Infrastructure development | 1 ☐ | 2 ☐ | 9 ☐ |
| C15 Provincial Land-Use strategic plan | 1 ☐ | 2 ☐ | 9 ☐ |
| C16 Provincial investment promotion policy | 1 ☐ | 2 ☐ | 9 ☐ |
| C17 Procedures and Form required for the coordination with the Government | 1 ☐ | 2 ☐ | 9 ☐ |
| C18 Public procurement opportunities | 1 ☐ | 2 ☐ | 9 ☐ |

C2. Have you ever submitted a request for information or documents that are not publicly available, from the provincial government?

1 ☐ Yes (answer C2.1-C2.2)　　0 ☐ No (answer C3)

C2.1. Did you receive all the information as requested?

1 ☐ Yes, I received all the information

2 ☐ No, I did not receive any information

3 ☐ I only received part of information requested

C2.2. Do you think companies like yours will he to pay any informal charge to the government officers to get those documents?

1 ☐ Yes　　　　　　　　0 ☐ No

C3. Did you have a chance to provide comments on the draft policy or regulations of the province?

1 ☐ Yes　　　　　　　　0 ☐ No

## D. Regulatory Burden

D1. How many times was your business inspected by the provincial authorities in 2018?

_____

D2. Compared to 2017, what was the frequency of inspection by the provincial government?

3 ☐ More often　　　　2 ☐ Less often　　　　1 ☐ No difference

D3. Which of the following agencies inspected and examined your firm in 2018?

| Document | Yes | No |
|---|---|---|
| Tax authority | 1 | 0 |
| Police authority | 1 | 0 |
| Industry and Commerce Authority | 1 | 0 |
| Line agency that issues operating license | 1 | 0 |
| Environment protection authority | 1 | 0 |
| Labor and social wealth-fare authority | 1 | 0 |
| Other, please specify _____ | 1 | 0 |

D4. Do you think the inspection of these authorities overlap or duplicate?

1 ☐ Yes                    0 ☐ No

D5. Do you think companies like yours will have to pay informal charges to the inspector for each inspection by the government?

1 ☐ Yes                    2 ☐ No

D6. How many days did it take you to renew your tax ID?
Total time spent (official working days) _____ days

D7. Please let us know how much did it cost you to renew your tax ID (TIN) in million LAK?
Total formal payment _____ Million Kip

D8. How many days did it take you to renew your operating license in 2018?
Total time spent (official working days) _____ days

D9. How much did it cost you to renew your operating license in 2018 (in Million LAK)?
Total formal payment _____ Million Kip

### E. Informal Charges

E1. On average, what percentages of YOUR REVENUE do firms like yours typically pay per year for informal charges to public officials?

_____

E2. Do you believe that the amount of informal charges that firms like yours pay when engaging with government are acceptable?

1 ☐ Yes                    0 ☐ No

E3. Do you think that it is common for the firms to pay extra "informal charges" to ensure that the business operation can be executed smoothly and easily?

1 ☐ Yes                    0 ☐ No

E4. Does the provincial government publish the informal charges/fees for their services to the public?

1 ☐ Yes 9 ☐ No

E5. Do you believe that it is common to negotiate your taxes in your business sector?

1 ☐ Yes 9 ☐ No

## F. Consistency in Policy Implementation

F1. Do you believe that the province implements central policy and regulation consistently?

1 ☐ Yes 0 ☐ No

F2. Do you believe that the different departments in the province work together well to support businesses?

1 ☐ Yes 0 ☐ No

F3. Are you subject to additional provincial regulations on business that differ from central regulations?

1 ☐ Yes (Answer F3.1) 0 ☐ No (answer F4)

F3.1 if yes, what is the impact of the additional provincial business regulations on your businesses?

1 ☐ Positive 2 ☐ Negative 3 ☐ The same

F4. Do you think the provincial government support the local private sector more than state-owned companies?

1 ☐ Yes 0 ☐ No 2 ☐ the same treatment

F5. Do you think the provincial government procurement contracts, land and other business resources mostly fall into the hands of enterprises that have strong connection with the provincial authorities?

1 ☐ Yes 0 ☐ No

## G. Business Friendliness of the Provincial Government

G1. Do you think the provincial government have positive attitude toward the private sector?

1 ☐ Yes 2 ☐ No

G2. Is the provincial government helpful to the private sector?

1 ☐ Yes 0 ☐ No

G3. Do you think the provincial government is willing to improve and apply new solutions to solve problems and constraints that the private sector is facing?

1 ☐ Yes          0 ☐ No

G4. Do you know about the Prime Minister Decree No 02 on improvement regulation and coordinating mechanism on doing business in the Lao PDR?

1 ☐ Yes (answer G5)      0 ☐ No (answer G7)

G5. Do you think Decree 02/PM would help improve the business environment in your province?

1 ☐ Yes (answer G5.1)    2 ☐ No (answer G5.2)    3 ☐ Do not know (answer G7)

G5.1 If yes, how does it improve business environment?

| Business environment | Yes | No |
|---|---|---|
| 1. Procedure of business establishment is more convenient and clearer (easier to start a company) | 1 | 0 |
| 2. Cost of business establishment decreased (lower cost of business registration) | 1 | 0 |
| 3. Entrepreneurs can access to business information (better access to business information) | 1 | 0 |
| 4. Government operation is more transparency (Greater transparency) | 1 | 0 |
| 5. Procedure of issuing operating license is faster and the fee is reasonable (faster issuance of operating licenses) | 1 | 0 |
| 6. Others (specify) _____ | 1 | 0 |

G5.2 If your answer no, why does it do not improve business environment?

| Business environment | Yes | No |
|---|---|---|
| 1. Procedure of business establishment does not much improvement | 1 | 0 |
| 2. Cost of business establishment remained high | 1 | 0 |
| 3. Entrepreneurs cannot access to business information | 1 | 0 |
| 4. Government operation is less transparency | 1 | 0 |
| 5. Procedure of issuing operating license is still complicated and high costs | 1 | 0 |
| 6. Others (specify)_____ | 1 | 0 |

G6. Which of the following actions would strengthen implementation of Decree 02?

1 ☐ Apply e-government to business registration (Multiple choice)

2 ☐ Apply e-tax filing and payment

3 ☐ Improve coordination between government agencies

4 ☐ Concrete timetable for reducing and simplifying business regulations and licenses

5 ☐ Other: _____

| G7. In the last year, did your firm use the following services in the province? If yes, please specify the providers? Services | No, don't use the service (1) | Yes, from which service provider | | |
|---|---|---|---|---|
| | | Provided by provincial agencies (2) | Provided by private sectors in the province (3) | Provided by the Private Organizations (Chamber of Commerce and Business Association) (4) |
| G71. Market information research | 0 | 1 | 2 | 3 |
| G72. Legal consultancy | 0 | 1 | 2 | 3 |
| G73. Recruitment | 0 | 1 | 2 | 3 |
| G74. Business matchmaking | 0 | 1 | 2 | 3 |
| G75. Trade promotion and trade fair / exhibition services | 0 | 1 | 2 | 3 |
| G76. Technology-related training program | 0 | 1 | 2 | 3 |
| G77. Training on Accounting and Finance | 0 | 1 | 2 | 3 |
| G78. Training on Business Administration | 0 | 1 | 2 | 3 |
| G79. Capacity building for the private sectors | 0 | 1 | 2 | 3 |
| 10. Others (Please identify _____) | 0 | 1 | 2 | 3 |

G8. Please rank the priority of the sections listed above– what should be prioritized by the provincial government to support the private sectors in the province? (1 means the highest priority and 5 means the lowest priority)

| | 1, highest priority | 2 | 3 | 4 | 5, lowest priority |
|---|---|---|---|---|---|
| Make it easier to start a business | 1 | 2 | 3 | 4 | 5 |
| Improve transparency and access to information | 1 | 2 | 3 | 4 | 5 |
| Reduce regulatory burden | 1 | 2 | 3 | 4 | 5 |
| Improve consistency in policy implementation | 1 | 2 | 3 | 4 | 5 |
| Be more friendly to private sector | 1 | 2 | 3 | 4 | 5 |

G8. Additional comments on improving business environment in your province?